Peaceful Sleep

A Practical Guide to
Stress-free Days and Tranquil Nights

*Including a Unique Bedtime Routine
that Really Works*

by

JAN SADLER

GATEWAY BOOKS, UK

First published in 1999
by GATEWAY BOOKS
The Hollies, Wellow,
Bath, BA2 8QJ

Distributed in the USA by
Access Publishers Network
6893 Sullivan Road, Grawn, MI 49637

Set in 11 on 14¹/₂pt Sabon by
Character Graphics (Taunton) Ltd,
Printed and bound by
Redwood Books of Trowbridge

Cover design by Synergie, Bristol
British Library Cataloguing-in Publication Data:
A catalogue record for this book is
available in the British Library

ISBN 1-85860-058-8

Contents

Peaceful Sleep by Jan Sadler

The techniques in *Peaceful Sleep* can be used alongside
conventional medical treatments.
If you have long-term insomnia, it may be advisable to
consult your doctor.

Introduction

If you find that achieving peaceful sleep is a major challenge in your life, you are not alone. Poor sleep is a very common experience, with most adults suffering from insomnia at some time in their lives. Loss of sleep can be the cause of great anxiety and distress, both for the sufferers and for those around them. The good news is that, with the methods described in this book, peaceful sleep will soon be yours. Your confidence in your sleep will grow and grow as you experience more and more peaceful, refreshing nights which will lead you into a natural and normal pattern of sleep.

Firstly, the techniques I describe in this book will give you the tools you need for use in the Peaceful Sleep Bedtime

Routine, a unique relaxation and visualisation programme to ease you gently into a deep and peaceful sleep at bedtime.

Secondly, the same simple techniques will enable you, in the longer term, to address lifestyle issues that may be the underlying cause of your sleeplessness. You will be able to build such a lifestyle for yourself that, in the future, deep and peaceful sleep will come automatically every night without necessarily having to use the Peaceful Sleep Bedtime Routine.

When your life is in balance and you live harmoniously with those around you, you sleep easily. By consistently using the practical and dynamic methods in this book, many other aspects of your life will show signs of positive and welcome change. A happier, more focused, confident and contented you will emerge. When you take care of your body and mind's needs in the way described, your whole life will become enriched and your reward will be a balanced, happy life full of wellbeing and vitality.

It is true to say that we grow towards that which we focus our minds upon. By focusing on how you would like your sleep to be and on ways of helping yourself towards that goal, you will achieve success. Read the Peaceful Sleep Ideal below and hold it in your mind as your goal, because what you choose to think about really does decide your reality. The Peaceful Sleep Ideal is more than a dream, it can come true for you – success is in your own hands and, with the help of this book, it will soon be yours.

The Peaceful Sleep Audiotape

You may like to know there is an audiotape which can be used alongside the book. Jan's soothing and relaxing voice will lead you through the Peaceful Sleep Bedtime Routine. This beautiful relaxation and visualisation allows you to drift gently and easily into a deep and peaceful sleep. You can obtain a copy of this outstanding tape by completing the order form at the back of the book.

Begin now, either with Side One of the audiotape or by reading the first chapter of this book.

Your Aim – the Peaceful Sleep Ideal

At bedtime, you feel pleasantly tired and ready for bed, with no thoughts or worries about the coming night and what it will bring.

You have no need for pills or alcohol to make you sleep.

In bed, you drift easily into a deep and peaceful sleep for the whole night through.

During the night you waken rarely, or, if woken, you fall asleep again effortlessly.

You awaken refreshed, full of energy and vitality, ready to begin the day with enthusiasm and vigour.

You enjoy this good, restorative sleep pattern on a regular basis.

This Peaceful Sleep Ideal is the normal, natural pattern of sleep and soon it will be yours.

This book will show you how to uncover your own inner strengths and abilities and how to develop a new peaceful and restful sleep habit, thus ensuring a true and long-lasting solution to the challenge of poor sleep. No matter what the cause of your sleep difficulties, you can be assured of success.

CHAPTER ONE

Stress-free Days for
Tranquil Nights

The Peaceful Sleep strategy for good sleep includes a number of easy-to-use techniques for you to practise during the day. When combined, these techniques comprise The Peaceful Sleep Bedtime Routine which you can use when you are actually in bed and want to go to sleep. You will need to take a little time out of your busy day to practise and use these techniques as well as using them at night. In addition to establishing the Peaceful Sleep Bedtime Routine, by using the techniques during the day you will ensure that your life is as calm, enjoyable and peaceful as possible because *the way you live your day affects the way you sleep at night.* Any challenges or upsets during the day can be handled so that you don't spend the night tossing and turning with unhelpful and disturbing thoughts whirling through your mind.

Stress of any kind is a major cause of unsettled sleep. Most of the difficulties around sleep are caused by challenges from the day that have not been addressed or resolved. Your brain takes advantage of the peace and quiet of the night to bring all these unfinished matters to the forefront of your attention. With no other distractions, your mind can churn the events of the day over and over, with all their frustrations and unresolved issues.

Sometimes sleeplessness can be the result of a short-term stressful event which caused a few nights of poor sleep. Those few sleep-disturbed nights may have triggered a downward spiral of anxiety and negative thinking about sleeping which led on to yet more poor sleep. As this pattern of poor sleep developed, the original cause may even have been forgotten. Then the stress from the anxiety and concern about sleeping itself becomes the main concern, rather than the cause of the insomnia. So a cycle is set up of poor sleep/worry about sleep/poor sleep ... and so on.

Stress is increasingly common in our modern lives. There have never been so many changes in society as there have been in our lifetime, and the pace of change is increasing all the time. Most of us find too much change and at too fast a pace extremely stressful. External forces, like change, or internal pressures that we put upon ourselves in this competitive world, can equally be responsible for increased stress. Today, even our children feel the pressure to achieve from a relatively young age.

Another source of strain is the information with which we are constantly bombarded, all of which requires some kind of response once it enters our consciousness. Much of the information we receive is negative – for example, there are many newspaper and television reports of disasters of many kinds about which we can do very little on a personal level.

However, most stress comes from the trivia upon which we

expend our energy each day and from incessant minor daily irritations. Tension comes particularly from the whole variety of electrical and mechanical equipment which is part of modern life, especially if it breaks down or frustrates us in some way. Over-stimulation in the day or evening can also contribute to a broken night's sleep. The adrenaline in your system, produced from over-excitement, inhibits sleep and, instead of being able to relax, you end up with a whirling mind and a restless, uncomfortable night.

We all need a certain amount of stress to give enjoyment and a zing to our lives and to release our creative powers. Without this we would soon become bored and unchallenged, which is as stressful as being overstretched. A definition of too much stress is when we end each day feeling as though there has been too much for us to do. We need to find a balance with just the right amount of stress to keep us lively and stimulated and yet able to cope with life's ups and downs without being over-extended.

You may not be able to solve or resolve any short or long-term stress in your life in an instant, but you can start the recovery process by seeking and using positive ways to reduce the stress in your life. When you take charge of your life in this beneficial way, you break the downward spiral of stress, negative feelings and disturbed sleep.

The Stress Response

When you are faced with an emergency situation, or when extra demands are placed upon you in any way, your body reacts automatically with a primitive 'stress response' by producing various hormones, including adrenaline, to help you cope with the situation. Adrenaline is an amazing chemical that enables you to take powerful and immediate action in a crisis. All humans and animals have built into their systems this stress response which functions automatically in order to protect them from danger by either staying to fight it out or by fleeing from the situation to safety (the 'flight or fight' reaction). In the past this enabled our ancestors to cope with life or death situations.

Your body systems go on 'Red Alert' when you perceive a threat to yourself. Imagine yourself as a warship under attack. You unleash your complete armoury to defend yourself – sirens scream, bells reverberate all over the ship, orders are issued over the tannoy system, all the crew speed to their posts, officers scour the radar for a sight of the danger and the weapons are primed and ready for action – all systems are 'GO'. The whole ship is concerned with protecting itself and few sailors are left to attend to the daily routines of the ship while the alert is in operation. When the danger is over, the ship quickly returns to its normal operating mode.

Something similar happens to you when you perceive a crisis and your body races into its 'Red Alert' and 'All Systems Go' procedure. For instance, suppose you are ambling along the pavement and your small daughter is dancing along just ahead of you. You are both relaxed and happy in the sunshine. The child sees a puppy over the road and turns to dash across to stroke it. You see a lorry hurtling down the road towards her and you realise that there is no way it can stop in time. Your primitive stress response fires immediately. Adrenaline and other chemicals flood your bloodstream causing your heart to pump harder. Your breathing speeds up, it's shallow and fast now, providing you with more oxygen for your heart, brain and muscles, your liver releases sugar and fats into your bloodstream to provide an immediate surge of energy, your senses become heightened and time seems almost to stand still, your muscles tighten and, in a split second, you spring into action. You hurl yourself forwards, scoop the child up and snatch her away from the wheels of the lorry as it thunders past. Afterwards, as your heart gradually returns to its normal speed and stops thumping in your chest, you wonder where the strength and speed came from for that life-saving rescue. You moved faster and more powerfully than you ever could normally. Once the danger has passed, your body quickly returns to normal. This kind of situation is where your primitive stress response is of life-saving value to you.

However, the stress response is not only triggered by life crises but by everyday challenges. For example, you have an appointment you really ought to keep and so you are keen to be on time. As you're going out of the door, keys in hand, the phone rings. You go back to answer it and find it's a double-glazing salesman. This irritates you and, after dealing with the call, you slam the phone down, rush out to the car and bang the front door behind you, muttering curses. The agitation is registered in your brain and it responds by initiating the stress response. Now adrenaline begins to flood your system although there is no actual danger to you in the events that have taken place. You get to the car and find you have shut your keys inside the house. Your brain senses your mounting frustration and sends the signals for the adrenaline to pump again and you feel hot and bothered. By the time you find the spare key under the stone in the front garden and have found your bunch of keys again you are ten minutes behind schedule. Adrenaline is pumping well by now, your neck is tight and your muscles tense as you shoot out of the drive into the traffic stream. You come to road work signs and your lane is stationary. There seems to be no reason for the stop light against you. You look at your watch, thump the wheel, sigh loudly, look again at your watch. It's hot in the car and you feel sweaty and uncomfortable. Your fists and jaw are clenched, your neck taut and your shoulders braced. You finally get out and pace up and down, feeling more and more stressed and frustrated. You think, "I'll never get there in time", over and over. Your brain receives the messages of distress from your thoughts and from your body language and the stress response is triggered again. Eventually the lights change and your traffic stream is allowed to drive on. You are certain you will be late for your appointment now. Every time you think of the appointment your anxiety increases, your muscles tighten some more, your heart pounds, more adrenaline floods your system and you feel the stress levels within you rising even higher. By the time you eventually arrive, your stomach is churning, you ache all over from muscle tension, you feel thoroughly agitated and have a splitting headache. Your body is full of a mix of chemicals and hormones brought about by the stress response being activated over and over without any chance to return to normal. During the whole episode there was never any danger to your life and the situation was not threatening in any way, the event was just filled with constant and increasing anxiety. Your brain cannot distinguish between real danger and imagined danger or anxiety. The stress response is activated every time you become agitated or fearful, regardless of the actual situation that provoked it.

The state of readiness the chemicals induced in your body cannot be maintained for long without depleting other internal processes. When the perceived pressure continues and the stress response is activated again and again without dissipation, you begin to feel ill in some way. When this occurs over a long period, the various organs become exhausted, resulting eventually in a breakdown of some kind, ranging from perhaps skin rashes or arthritis to heart disease or a stroke – and almost certainly sleep patterns will have been disturbed. The stress response chemicals inhibit 'sleep hormones' and so, if there is an adrenaline build-up during the day, it will hinder sleep at night.

The stress response is initiated by many different situations, real and, as mentioned, imaginary anxieties. Fear and anxiety are the biggest stressors of all. Fear, unlike external threats, is in the mind – and so it can come within our influence. The series of events which led up to the appointment being missed and high stress levels experienced could have been handled in a far more constructive way which may have avoided such an escalation of the stress response.

Your subconscious mind operates in a very simple way – it takes on board all the information it receives at face value, regardless of whether it is true or not. For example, if it receives the information that a situation is giving anxiety, your subconscious mind doesn't question the message, it just acts upon it and immediately fires the stress response, sending adrenaline shooting around your body, priming it to a state of readiness. If you think, as in the missed appointment scenario, "I'll be late", "I'll never get there in time", "What will they think of me?", "I'll lose the chance to ..." or any other anxious and negative thoughts, your subconscious mind will accept those thoughts unconditionally and they will become your reality. This is because *we move towards whatever we choose to think about.* Your brain constantly tries to close the gap between the information it is receiving and what is actually taking place in the real world. So, by saying to yourself, "I'll never get there in time", you make it more likely that you won't. This is because, as your agitation grows, you will also increase the probability of causing yourself further hold-ups through accidents or mistakes. Altogether an unsatisfactory experience.

Now if, instead, you were to tell yourself, "There is plenty of time. Life is not an emergency. There will be lots of other opportunities for me", your subconscious mind would tell your body to relax and go with the experience. There would be no sense of danger or anxiety coming from the situation and so your brain would be more likely to activate the release of endorphins, its own 'feelgood' chemicals, rather than adrenaline, the stress response chemical. The thoughts you think have an instant effect upon your body and you would immediately feel calmer and more relaxed. Amazingly, life would start to flow, and you would be more certain to arrive on or near your appointment time. Even if you were late, you would not arrive flustered and stressed-out with a thumping headache, but in a far more philosophical mood, thinking, "Oh well, there will be plenty more opportunities. Next time I'll leave earlier and make sure I have everything I need with me." You could add an extra note of positivity to the situation by using the additional time as a gift to practise some of the stress-reducing techniques outlined in this book.

You have seen how a series of events, the lost keys and the traffic jam experience, could be handled in different ways, one leading to a full-blown stress response experience and the other leading to a calm, more ordered and constructive situation. The only difference between the two versions is *what you told yourself*.

I am sure you can see how this knowledge about how to handle events can help you with your sleep. When you have a poor night, or are concerned about what will happen in the night ahead, it's very easy to concentrate on thoughts such as, "I'll never get to sleep", "I hardly slept a wink last night", or "I'll feel awful in the morning".

But, you may say, those thoughts come to my mind automatically – and you would be right. Thoughts *do* come into your mind automatically. One of the functions of the brain is to produce thoughts. You can't control the thoughts that come into your mind. However, those thoughts are not some kind of power in charge of you, they are produced for you to deal with as you will. *You*, the inner 'You', are the power behind the thoughts. *You* are in charge of your thoughts. *You* are the Thinker in your mind. Your mind produces a new thought every second or so but *You*, the Thinker behind the thoughts, can intervene. You can stop those thoughts in their tracks, and then choose thoughts of your own, thoughts that are more creative and fruitful for you. There is *always* a choice in the matter of thoughts. You can always choose not to concentrate upon or to follow downbeat thoughts.

As an example of this, think for a moment about what happens when you read this book. As you read, your thoughts will be constantly changing. In addition to making sense of the words on the page, a whole variety of thoughts will float through your mind from time to time. You may wonder what you are going to eat later, you may think for a moment about how warm or cold it is getting, another thought might arrive about an exciting event next week, the next thought might be a worry thought about a situation you are involved in, and so on. Some of the thoughts are neutral, some are positive and some are negative.

As all these thoughts come to your mind, you may notice that it is easy to dismiss many of them. For instance, you don't necessarily spend a long time thinking about how warm it is, other thoughts soon replace that thought. You can also learn to dismiss negative, unwanted thoughts in the same way. Those thoughts, too, can be allowed to float through your mind without affecting you.

Because your thoughts influence your physical and emotional states, and your thoughts are within your control, it makes sense that, if you change your thoughts, you can change the way your body functions and change the way you are feeling. Just because a certain thought comes into your mind it doesn't mean that you have to believe that thought or take any notice of that thought. So, if your mind produces thoughts such as, "I'll never be able to go to sleep tonight", it does not mean that this is what will happen, unless you *choose* to believe it. You can also choose to dismiss the thought and deliberately replace it with a more supportive thought, such as, "I sleep peacefully at night". No matter for how long you have been believing your negative thoughts, you always have the freedom to change those thoughts for new ones. Every moment is a new beginning for you.

Concentrating on more uplifting and positive thoughts doesn't mean that negative thoughts will never enter your mind again. They will continue to do so but, as time goes by and you become more aware of your thought processes, the constant barrage of negative thoughts you may receive will gradually reduce and be replaced by the automatic production of more positive thoughts.

In order to become more aware of your thoughts and their content it will be useful for you to carry out the next exercises.

Two Thought Awareness Exercises

Choose to complete either or both of the following exercises to give an awareness of the content of your thoughts.

What you need:
- a piece of paper or a notebook and a pen or pencil
- a countdown timer (a kitchen timer is fine)

Ten Minute Mindwatch

Find a place where you will be undisturbed for about a quarter of an hour. Set your timer for ten minutes. Make sure you are comfortable. Focus for a moment on your breath as it flows in and out of your body. Let it become just a little slower and a little deeper. Then start the timer and just allow thoughts to enter your consciousness. As they come to your attention, jot them down.

Don't try to think about anything in particular, let thoughts materialise on their own. Above all, don't be judgmental about the contents of the thoughts. Some of them may be along the lines of, "This is absurd", "How will this help me to sleep?" and so on. That doesn't matter, just write them down. This exercise is for your eyes only and all that needs concern you is becoming aware of your thoughts. After the first few self-conscious thoughts, you will find that other thoughts begin to surface.

When the timer rings, look at your list and see what you can discover from the type of thoughts that came into your mind. Were they mostly slanted towards the positive or negative?

Did you find many critical thoughts? Were the thoughts principally about the past or the future? Were there any thoughts directly concerned with your sleep?

There are no 'right' or 'wrong' answers to this exercise. The exercise is merely to raise your awareness about your thoughts and the type of thoughts you think.

Half-Hourly Thought Catching Exercise

Set your timer for half an hour and then carry on with your tasks in the normal way. When the timer goes off, jot down what you were thinking at the time. Do this again throughout the morning, the afternoon or the evening.

Again, after you've gathered a page or so of thoughts, take time to analyse them in the same way as in the Ten Minute Mindwatch exercise.

After carrying out either or both of these thought awareness exercises you will be more familiar with the type of thoughts that pass through your mind. The results of your thought catching exercise may be quite surprising to you. Whatever the results, remember that in the next chapter you are going to find out exactly how to change any negative thought patterns to more positive and constructive thought patterns.

Summary

1. The quality of your sleep is a reflection of the way you live your day.

2. Stress and over-stimulation can contribute to a broken night's sleep.

3. The 'stress response' is initiated by anxiety and fear.

4. Fear is in the mind and so is within your influence.

5. You can reduce the effects of the 'stress response' by changing the way you view events.

6. Thoughts are powerful. Become aware of your thoughts and their contents.

7. You can learn to change your thoughts to those that are more self-supportive.

8. Use the two thought-awareness exercises to 'catch' your thoughts.

CHAPTER TWO

Developing Your Inner Powers

Positive Self-Talk

Redirecting Your Self-talk

In this chapter you will discover how to use during the day the various techniques that, together, combine to make up the Peaceful Sleep Bedtime Routine – the routine you will follow at night when you want to go to sleep. These are the techniques that will help you to build a balanced, relaxed and harmonious life in which you cope with stress with ease.

In the last chapter we thought about the place negative self-talk has in producing stress and poor sleep. Now it's time to discover the power of positive thinking.

If you have a difficult night your thoughts may tend to

become very negative. You may also become anxious about the following night, wondering what will happen and how you will sleep. This anxiety about losing sleep can be the main cause of losing yet more sleep. Sometimes, you may find that when you go to bed your mind is racing, with thoughts whirling round and round in your head. You may keep repeating the same thoughts or replaying some event from the day over and over in your mind. These are the times to step in and use the Peaceful Sleep Programme of 'STOP/CANCEL/ CHANGE!' which follows shortly, in order to banish negative thoughts and to quieten your mind.

You were not born with negative thoughts in your mind. Your negative thought patterns were learned from your experiences since childhood, both pleasant and unpleasant, and from the behaviour towards you of those around you. Your learned thought patterns developed from what was said to you, or what you thought was implied by what was said to you, by your parents, teachers, relatives and any of the many other people with whom you came into contact. The good intention of these adults was, of course, to teach you how to behave or perform in various situations. Unfortunately, their intentions were open to misinterpretation. For example, if you behaved in a way that was undesirable – say, snatching a toy from another child – you may have been told you were 'bad' to do that and the adult may have appeared to be angry with you. You may have inferred from this that *you* were bad and unloved whereas, in reality, it was your action that was unacceptable, not *you*.

Now, if you are capable of learning negative thought patterns, you are equally capable of learning more productive thought patterns and uncovering your innate positivity. With practice, it will gradually become second nature to you to seek and find positive thought patterns which are more uplifting and supporting for you. Meanwhile, when you notice a negative thought or find yourself dwelling on anxious, downbeat thoughts, have an attitude of compassion and understanding towards yourself.

Remember that you do not flourish and grow in an atmosphere of criticism but in a supporting, loving climate.

When you are watching for unhelpful thoughts, be particularly on the lookout for thoughts that are restricting and reflect a limiting option – words such as 'never', 'must', 'ought, 'should', 'always'. These words are self-defeating and repressing and often a 'put-down' of either yourself or someone else. Again, these are blocking ideas that you have picked up over many years. Say to yourself, "I can let these thoughts go, I have no need of them". You can then allow the thoughts to float away, and turn to finding more constructive thoughts. You always have a choice, and each and every moment can be a fresh start for you. When you choose to pursue constructive, upbeat and nourishing thoughts they will lead you away from the likelihood of the stress response being fired and allow 'feelgood' endorphins to be released. Your self-talk is *yours* to direct as you choose.

The 'STOP/CANCEL/CHANGE!' Technique to Quieten your Mind

The easy-to-use 'STOP/CANCEL/CHANGE!' technique is the starting point of the Peaceful Sleep Programme and is the key to arresting mental chatter of any kind. It is the means of banishing that discouraging negative inner voice which, on occasions, may persist inside your head. It is also the answer to finding a peaceful night's sleep. This is what to do –
When you notice you are thinking in a negative way, say firmly to yourself, using a strong, convincing tone, either inside your head or out aloud:

"STOP!"

Be really firm and unshakable in your intention. Your mind is going to stop what it is doing, and that is final – you won't stand for any more nonsense! You will find the immediate effect

*is an astounded silence in your mind. Your mind will be shocked
at being spoken to in this way, as it normally carries on producing one thought after another without hindrance from anyone
or anything. Now the 'You' behind your thoughts has come to
the fore and shown it who is in charge. Now 'You' are in control again, albeit for a moment. Maintain the advantage by
swiftly saying to yourself:*

"CANCEL that thought"

By saying CANCEL *that thought you are deliberately going to erase
the thought and the ideas behind the thought, thus making dou-
bly sure it doesn't arise again. If you like, you can reinforce the
idea that the thought is cancelled by imagining a large board with
the thought written upon it. Now imagine wiping that thought
away with a board-wiper. Really 'see' clearly in your mind the
picture of your arm and hand rubbing the thought away until it
has gone from sight, leaving the board clean and shining.*

All of this takes only a split second or so and will allow you
to break away from the potentially stressful situation and start
again on a new, positive track.

When you say your 'STOP' and 'CANCEL that thought' you have
complete control of your mind. This breathing space you have
created for yourself needs to be maintained in order for you not
to slip back into more negative thoughts. Now that you have control it is essential that you remain in control. The next step in the
'STOP/CANCEL/CHANGE' technique is to CHANGE the old thought for
a brand new thought that is more constructive and supportive.
This type of positive thought or sentence is called an affirmation.
You now need to concentrate on these new, beneficial thoughts to
make certain that self-defeating thoughts are kept away.

Daily Affirmations

Immediately you have said to yourself "STOP" and then "CAN-
CEL that thought", quickly and deliberately slot in some new

positive thoughts. Repeat the new thoughts over and over until you are sure you have control and feel calm and uplifted. At first they may feel uncomfortable for you but keep going, you will soon begin to feel the benefit and the statements *will* be true for you. You can select three or four from the following affirmations if you wish:

"I am calm and confident."

"I can handle this."

"I love and approve of myself."

"I am the power and authority in my life."

"I concentrate on the good in my life."

"I am patient with myself and with others."

"Today is a good day. Today is MY day."

"Be still, this will pass." (Excellent during times
     of stress)

"I let go thoughts about the past and thoughts about
     the future."

It is most helpful to have your list of chosen affirmations ready prepared for use. You could write them on individual cards to make it easy to learn them. Repeat them as often as you can during the day to imprint them upon your mind. Use any of the above affirmations or, best of all, make up your own. When you create you own, make sure the phrases are easy to remember and to the point. This will ensure that they are easily accepted by your subconscious mind. For affirmations to be effective, they need to have an outcome you 100 per cent desire to happen. When you make an affirmation you state or affirm that something you wish for is already here and taking effect right now. You don't have to *believe* the positive sentence initially. By saying your affirmation in a convincing tone of voice, either aloud or inside your head, you fool your subconscious mind into absorbing it. Rather like a computer, your subconscious mind always takes on board whatever messages it receives, whether the messages are true, false, negative or positive. The messages are passed on and your body and your feelings respond accordingly. In the long term you can gradually change the way you think and the way you feel by continuously feeding to your mind affirmations which are supporting, uplifting, and life-enhancing.

The previous affirmations are for your general use during the day, to boost your confidence and introduce an atmosphere of calm into your life. Remember that how you live your day affects the way you sleep at night.

The Peaceful Sleep Affirmation

The Peaceful Sleep affirmation is the affirmation that you will use specifically for sleep throughout the Peaceful Sleep programme. As we found above, the subconscious mind acts upon what it is repeatedly told, and so, instead of feeding it negative, worrying thoughts about your sleep, you are going to change to the positive thought that you sleep peacefully all night long every night. You will use this positive affirmation despite the fact that it may not necessarily be true at the moment. You are *not* deceiving yourself, you are giving yourself instructions or directions for your subconscious mind to follow and bring to reality.

The affirmation to use for peaceful sleep is:

"Peaceful sleep. When I say 'peaceful sleep' I fall asleep easily and sleep right through the night."

So, when you notice a negative or worrying thought coming into your mind about your sleep, overcome it by immediately saying your new Peaceful Sleep affirmation.

Take a small piece of card upon which to write this affirmation. When you read it, read it through twice on each occasion. On the second reading, to reinforce the affirmation even more, alter it slightly and say to yourself in a totally positive way,

"<u>YES</u> I <u>DO</u> When I say 'peaceful sleep' I <u>DO</u> fall asleep
easily and I <u>DO</u> sleep right through the night."

Read the card over and over during the day, either out loud or
inside your head. Do this as often as you can during the day,
five, ten, fifteen, twenty times or more. When you say the
words, repeat them slowly, with real feeling, really thinking
about what the words mean, *as though they are actually true
for you right now.* The ideas in the affirmation will gradually
be accepted by your subconscious mind.

Diaphragmatic Breathing

As you already discovered when you were reading about the
stress response, if you are in an emergency situation, such as
running to catch a train or to save a child from dashing into the
road, your breathing becomes very short and shallow. This is
because your body is attempting to provide you with more oxygen to give your heart, brain and muscles an instant surge of
energy. In a situation where you are under ongoing strain this
'flight or fight' stress response often takes place inappropriately
and on a more continuous basis. In these circumstances, the
extra energy is not burnt up physically with activity, as it would
be in a genuine crisis situation, and the stress chemicals are not
dissipated. Instead they accumulate in your body, where they
can produce physical symptoms such as headaches, tingling
hands, limbs or face, cramps, dizziness, fatigue, chest pains and
digestive upsets. The shorter, shallower breathing which accom-
panies the stress response serves only, in this situation, to make
you feel more and more anxious. Unfortunately, many of us
breathe habitually in this shallow way which can, in itself, cause
the body and the mind to become stressed. Either of these pat-

*Peaceful Sleep – when I say "peaceful sleep" I fall asleep
easily and sleep right through the night*

terns of behaviour can cause a downward spiral of increasing stress, worry about the physical symptoms and, as a result, yet more physical symptoms, all of which can then, of course, be reflected in the way you sleep. As you read earlier, the way you live your day affects the way you sleep at night.

There is a simple answer to these predicaments. In one word, your *breath*. Yes, your breath can become your ally and friend and begin to work *with* you instead of against you. Used in the right way, breathing is a wonderful activity that will come to your aid, not only during the day to help control any stress in your life, but also during the night when you wish to drift into peaceful sleep.

In the USA, a cardiologist, Herbert Benson, discovered the antidote to the 'flight or fight' stress response. He called it the 'relaxation response'. In his research he found that the conscious use of breath can have a positive input in various functions of the body, such as lowering the heart rate, lowering blood pressure, improving circulation and improving the immune function. The 'relaxation response' comes about when we use any relaxation or meditation method in which the breathing becomes deep and slow. This kind of breathing is called diaphragmatic breathing. Your diaphragm is a large dome-shaped muscle attached all round the lower part of your rib cage, like a floor dividing your chest from your abdomen. On an in-breath the diaphragm moves downwards, the abdomen is pushed out by the incoming breath and the whole of your chest expands outwards at both the front and the back and also sideways. On an out-breath the diaphragm returns upwards and the abdomen falls as the old, used air is expelled.

Diaphragmatic breathing has major benefits to you. The oxygen taken during the deep in-breath feeds and regenerates all the cells of your body. When you breathe out, all the impurities from the cleansed cells are expelled from your body. Diaphragmatic breathing nourishes your whole system and allows for the optimum function of many other parts of your body. Deep, diaphragmatic breathing is also the key to all stress relief because it helps relieve tension from your muscles, relaxes your mind and allows your body's own 'feelgood' chemicals, endorphins, to flow. Your breath is completely dependable; when all around you may be falling about, it is always there, available to you to use. Your breath can, almost miraculously, transform the way you feel. When you practise deep diaphragmatic breathing, you quickly begin to feel peaceful, serene, relaxed, full of wellbeing and 'centred', that is, calmly and firmly earthed in the present moment. Worries and fears float away and are brought into perspective.

We mostly tend to take our breathing for granted, not paying attention to it at all. After all, it functions by itself whether or not we take any notice of it; we don't have to *think* about how to breathe in order for our next breath to arrive. It is, however, a function that we *can* take hold of and use deliberately to our great advantage.

Take yourself through this diaphragmatic 'breathing treat' five, six, seven times or more throughout the day until you have retrained yourself to breathe the diaphragmatic way on a regular basis.

Diaphragmatic Breathing Practice: 'STOP' and Breathe, the 'Two-Sighs' Method

First of all, make yourself as comfortable as you can, wherever you are, standing, sitting or lying down. Loosen your clothing around your middle.

You might like begin by using a slight variation of your 'STOP/CANCEL/CHANGE' *technique. Say,*

"STOP!"

firmly to yourself, either inside your head or out aloud. Be

Peaceful Sleep – when I say "peaceful sleep" I fall asleep easily and sleep right through the night

quietly firm. You are instructing yourself to call a halt to what you are doing and thinking, to gain a moment's peace and quiet from your body and mind, so ... 'CANCEL' those automatic thoughts and fidgety habits and 'CHANGE' direction on to a new track. Now 'You', the real 'You', are in control again to do as YOU decide. On this occasion, instead of changing to positive affirmations, you are going to concentrate on your breathing instead and fill the space you have created with two lovely deep relaxing breaths taken in a special way.

So, having said "STOP!" to yourself to quieten your mind, turn your attention to your breathing; breathing through your nose ... Focus your attention on your abdomen and just notice its rise and fall as your breath flows in and out. You can allow your breathing to become slightly deeper and slightly slower.

And now, on your next out-breath, imagine that your breath is travelling from the top of your head down to your abdomen, and let it out with a gentle sigh, like this ... aaahh- hhh ... and, at the same time, let your shoulders relax, let your shoulders go ... Let all the breath out right down to the very last bit of air. Feel your abdomen contract as the old stale air is pushed out. Close your mouth and let the in-breath come of its own accord. Notice how your diaphragm pops up with the intake of breath. The sigh encourages diaphragmatic breathing to begin. As you expel all the old air, a new deep breath of oxygen-rich air is automatically taken in.

Breathe like this once more and, this time, imagine that your out-breath is travelling from the top of your head, down through your body, right down to your toes and into the earth. With a sigh ... aaahhhhhh ... let even more air out, let your feet sink into the ground, let go ... and feel even more relaxed.

And now continue to breathe quietly and normally through your nose, enjoying the relaxing effect you have brought about for a few moments more. Your breathing will now be from your abdomen and making full use of your diaphragm. This 'two-sighs' breathing kick-starts diaphragmatic breathing into being. It ensures that you are breathing correctly from the abdomen and not from the chest.

Be still and just enjoy a few moments of deep and natural breathing through your nose. Deep diaphragmatic breathing can release all tension and stress and will set you up with the right frame of mind for the day.

Practise this quick and easy 'STOP and Breathe' technique often during the day to avoid a build-up of stress – for instance, when you're waiting for something, every time you're in the bathroom or when you look at the clock to check the time. Choose your own 'natural breaks'. You could even set a timer for every hour and then 'STOP and Breathe'. Use these regular occasions to take the opportunity to practise your diaphragmatic breathing. In this way you will develop a new habit of breathing more deeply and slowly throughout the day. You will give yourself a few moments of peace and calm in your busy life, which will allow you to return to your task refreshed and in a more relaxed and controlled way. You will be more able to let go of minor worries and to keep the 'fight or flight' reaction at bay.

At first you may find this breathing a little strange, but keep practising and it will soon feel more natural to you. Remember to concentrate on the out-breath, exhaling as much as you can without forcing. The in-breath will take care of itself and will automatically be deep and easy.

The more you practise, the easier you will find it to switch to your deep diaphragmatic breathing as soon as you start to feel stressed in any way. If you find yourself in a difficult situation or thinking unhelpful thoughts, remember to 'STOP!' and take these two relaxing breaths to bring yourself back to feeling in control, calm and centred. This method of breathing is

Peaceful Sleep – when I say "peaceful sleep" I fall asleep easily and sleep right through the night

an essential tool for you to use at night. It can become one of the first things for you to do when you go to bed, to lead you into a peaceful night's sleep. Each time you practise during the day it makes it easier and easier for you to use the techniques successfully at bedtime.

You could add some affirmations, if you like, to your breathing practice, to reinforce the benefits of the diaphragmatic breathing. Choose from the following or make up your own:

> *I concentrate on my breathing."*
> *"Be peaceful.............be still."*
> *"Relax...........this will pass.'*
> *"Breathe out...........and let go............."*
> *"My breathing is slow and steady."*
> *"I let go, I float and flow through time."*
> *"I take one moment at a time and concentrate on what I*
>   *am doing now."*
> *"I let go any thoughts of the past and the future."*
> *(On in-breath) "I breathe in and relax ..." (On out-breath)*
>   *"I breathe out and let go.... "*
> or simply,
> *"Peace", "Relax,"* or any other comforting words.

Relaxation

The diaphragmatic breathing method leads on quite naturally to the relaxation process itself. For a relaxation session, you sit or lie down and relax completely for about fifteen to twenty minutes, entering a deeply peaceful and relaxed state of body and mind. The 'relaxation response' will calm you and, as you let go of any tension, give you relief from any aches and pains. When you relax deeply, you not only release tight muscles, you may also sometimes release emotions and thoughts you have been holding on to. If this happens, allow those thoughts and feelings to come to the surface and let them go. Once they arise and are experienced, they are released and finished with. Be grateful for this opportunity to release inner tension.

Relaxation skills are an essential element of the Peaceful Sleep programme. Deep relaxation helps your body in many ways. It releases muscle tension, enhances your body's natural healing processes, releases endorphins (your body's own natural painkillers and 'feelgood' agents) and gives your body and mind deep, natural feelings of peace and comfort. Treat yourself to as many relaxation sessions as you can during the day.

The following Peaceful Sleep Body Scan relaxation is one of my favourite ways to let go of all tension and to feel deeply peaceful and calm. It happily combines affirmation techniques with relaxation and is also simple and totally adaptable. The rhythm and pattern of the words is very repetitive and comforting and is ideally soporific when used last thing at night for slipping into a peaceful sleep.

There are various ways you could practise the Body Scan. You could tape-record the script below, or read it through until you have memorised most of it, or ask someone to read the script to you. Take your time and, where there are dots, leave pauses to enjoy the relaxation.

The Peaceful Sleep Body Scan

In the Body Scan you are going to talk, in your mind, to different parts of your body, allowing them to relax and let go in turn. You will allow soothing warmth and relaxation to spread around your body when you place your attention on each part of your body and allow it to soften and relax. The key word here is 'allow' – you just give the instructions and allow whatever happens to happen. The relaxation will come

Peaceful Sleep – when I say "peaceful sleep" I fall asleep easily and sleep right through the night

by just *thinking* about it. There's nothing to *do*, you need only to think gently about each part of your body and, as you do so, say to that part, on an out-breath, *"Relax........"*

First of all, make sure you are comfortable and warm, and either sitting with your head supported or lying down. You need to be undisturbed for about ten minutes or so.

Begin by placing your attention on your feet. Then allow relaxation to spread around your feet – to your toes, your heels, the bottom of each foot, the top of each foot and your ankles. Feel your feet relax, and be just a little more comfortable. Just let the tensions go ... On an out-breath, say to your feet *"Relax ..."*

Now move on to your lower legs. Let your lower legs relax, ... let them feel heavy and warm ... and on an out-breath say *"Relax ..."* to your lower legs ...

And now think about your upper legs. Let the relaxation spread all around your upper legs ... and on an out-breath say *"Relax ..."* to them.

Allow the relaxation to spread into your lower back, all around your lower back ... and on an out-breath say *"Relax ..."* to your lower back ...

And now take your attention to your abdomen. Feel how soft and warm your abdomen is ... and say *"Relax ... "* to your abdomen ...

Let the relaxation flow into your upper back, your chest and your shoulders ... let your shoulders sink down into the surface beneath you. Feel the whole area relax and let go ... and on an out-breath say *"Relax ..."*

Now take your attention slowly down each arm, right to your fingertips. Let each arm feel heavy and relaxed from your shoulder to the tips of your fingers ... and say *"Relax ..."*

Focus on your neck, let it feel soft and free ... and on an out-breath say *"Relax ..."* to your neck ...

And then allow relaxation to spread up into your whole

head and face ... and say *"Relax ... "* to your head and face.

Your forehead is wide, smooth and relaxed ... Your eyes are peaceful and all the tiny muscles around your eyes are relaxed. ... Your whole face is filled with relaxation, it is serene and peaceful ... and on an out-breath say *"Relax ..."* to your face ...

Your whole body is beautifully relaxed and heavy....you feel very peaceful and at ease ... Say *"Relax ..."* to your whole body ...

And now, for a few moments, just *enjoy* the sensations you have created ... and then become aware of the surface beneath you ... stretch your fingers and toes and, when you're ready, slowly and gently open your eyes and come back to the room, feeling totally relaxed, peaceful and calm ...

When you begin to 'let go' at the start of the relaxation process you may become aware of all kinds of sensations from your body, a little localised twitching or feelings of warmth and heaviness as your body settles down. These sensations are not unpleasant and are best ignored, they will soon pass, as will any emotions that may arise momentarily as you begin to relax. Just be thankful of the opportunity to release them. As you relax more and more, you enter a really peaceful and relaxed state where your body seems to float away from you and thoughts and feelings become quiet.

Practise the Body Scan every day, as you will then be able to use it successfully as part of the Peaceful Sleep Bedtime Routine. If you have recorded the Body Scan or if someone reads it to you, remember that it is important to practise both with and without listening to it on tape or having it read to you. You can do this by talking yourself through the Body Scan, just focusing on parts of the body in turn. There's no

Peaceful Sleep – when I say "peaceful sleep" I fall asleep easily and sleep right through the night

need to use the same words that I did, just use the general idea of going around your body, saying *"Relax ..."* to each part in turn. Take plenty of time, don't rush it. You can use any parts of your body you like, adding more parts of you wish, especially any parts you feel could do with a little extra help. You don't have to go through the Body Scan in the same order as I did here, although it is helpful to start with your feet and work gradually and slowly up through your body, finishing with your head and face and finally your whole body. Each time you practise, you will gain more from the ideas. The more you practise, the more proficient you will become, making it easier and easier to slip into a deep, peaceful sleep at night. When you practise your relaxing Body Scan, sit or lie down with your clothing loosened in a quiet place where you will be undisturbed for twenty minutes or so.

You will find you need to be quite disciplined to achieve regular relaxation or visualisation practice. The fifteen to twenty minutes you need is not very long but it is surprising how difficult it can be to find this amount of time for yourself, even when you know it is to your own advantage. So don't underrate your mind's ability to sabotage your good intentions. Be firm with yourself and make your relaxation time an absolute priority.

If you live in a busy household, explain to your family and friends that you need to set aside twenty minutes or so a day as part of a new programme to help you sleep. This will ensure they are supportive of your effort – and they will surely appreciate the new relaxed 'you'.

At first, if you are very tired, it is possible that you may fall asleep whilst you are relaxing. If this happens, that's fine, but remember that sleep taken during the day will mean less sleep at night. Sleep itself is different from deep relaxation. Try to time your relaxation session for when you are not so tired that you fall asleep.

Remember that practice of any technique is essential. The more you rehearse the greater the benefits will be, just as in a work-out where the more you train the fitter and more flexible you become. The ability to relax at will is hugely rewarding with life-long benefits, not the least of which is to gain peaceful sleep with effortless ease.

Visualisation

The relaxation response is rather like a gateway through which you enter a different realm, one of almost unlimited potential. You enter a peaceful world where you can use the powers of your imagination to add another dimension to your health and happiness and to further ensure your peaceful sleep. In this inner world, using your own imaginative abilities in the skill of visualisation, it is actually possible to transform the way your body functions. Dr. Herbert Benson found that the practitioners of a form of yoga could raise their external body temperature by more than ten degrees, although their inner body temperature remained at its usual level. It has been found that, in experiments and in practice, people can raise their body temperature simply by 'thinking warm'. The power of suggestion is so strong that if, for example, when deeply relaxed, someone was told that the object they were given to touch was a red-hot iron, their skin could turn red as though burnt or could sometimes even blister.

This ability to use your imagination so vividly and effectively can be turned to your own great advantage when you are seeking ways to help promote peaceful sleep. The exciting technique of visualisation can be used by everyone, even though you may think you don't have that kind of imaginative power. It is a skill that may be lying forgotten or dormant within you. As a child you would have used your imagination in your play or when day-dreaming. As you grew older, you may have been encouraged to use the logical, reasoning left

Peaceful Sleep – when I say "peaceful sleep" I fall asleep easily and sleep right through the night

side of your brain for formal schoolwork at the expense of the imaginative, creative right side of your brain. With practice, this ability can be restored and nourished and will then allow you to use some imaginative visualisation techniques to create the changes you desire in order to generate a more fulfilling lifestyle and to promote peaceful sleep at night. Although you may not recognise it as such, you already have some skill with visualisation.

Try this experiment. Take your time, relax and just notice what happens:

Close your eyes, take a deeper breath in and let it out slowly and fully, then breathe normally.

Now take a moment or two to think of eating your favourite food.

When you thought of your favourite food, did you see a picture in your mind? Could you taste the food? People bring their memories out from their subconscious mind in different ways. You may have had a fleeting picture in your mind of your food; you may have smelt it, tasted it or perhaps re-experienced the emotions of a particular time in your past when you ate it. For example, you may have recalled the feelings of excitement you had when you were eating your favourite food at a special celebration dinner. You may have had a full picture in your mind of the whole scene, or you may have just sensed the food in some way that you can't identify. In whatever way you recalled your favourite food, that is your imagination in action. We all find our own ways of using our imagination to bring our memories to the fore. Whatever way you remembered the food is perfectly fine and is all that is required to bring the powerful and creative energies of visualisation to your life.

When you deliberately use your imagination to influence an aspect of your life you are giving messages and instructions to your subconscious mind. The subconscious mind accepts whatever messages it receives without question. Questioning is part of the logical side of your brain which is not involved during visualisation processes when you are relaxed. Think back to the example of the people who thought they were being burned – their logical mind had 'switched off' during the relaxation and was not questioning whether or not someone really would try to burn them; their subconscious mind just accepted what it was told was happening. As a result, their mind sent the message to the skin that it had been burnt and the skin reacted in the way that it would have if it had really been burnt. If what you want can be visualised clearly in your mind, the reality will follow, it is as straightforward as that.

Whether the pictures in your mind are of real or imaginary events or objects, it makes no difference to the way your body and mind react to the images. So, when you visualise yourself as being a healthy, strong person it is not self-*deception* but self-*direction*. You are visualising the desired outcome, and we always grow towards *anything* about which we constantly think and visualise. So, even when you are tired, see yourself *always* as being full of energy and vitality, tell yourself, *"I am full of energy"*, and you are more likely to overcome your feelings of tiredness.

Practising Visualisation Skills

Visualisation is most enjoyable and can be great fun. Like any other skill, your visualisation skill will improve with practice and will continue to improve as you gain confidence in your ability to visualise. Take some time to imagine the short scenes below. You don't have to **try** to do or see anything, as you can't **force** images and sensations upon yourself. So however you get to sense the scene, that's fine.

First of all, allow yourself to relax. Close your eyes and take a deeper breath than normal, then let out a lovely long out-breath.

Peaceful Sleep – when I say "peaceful sleep" I fall asleep easily and sleep right through the night

Read item No. 1, then close your eyes again and imagine the scene. Do this for each suggestion. Take your time and just note what happens when you think of each scene described.

1. *You see a tiny aeroplane flying very high above the white fluffy clouds in the blue sky. There is a vapour trail coming from behind the plane. The plane moves slowly across the sky and soon all that is left is the vapour trail, gradually becoming fainter and fainter.*

2. *You are in the park taking an early morning run. Feel the sensation in your body of running. The birds are singing, the air is fresh and cool on your skin. The early morning sun glows through the trees.*

3. *You are on a tropical beach with white sand, palm trees, a deep blue sky and a turquoise-blue sea, with the sound of gulls crying as they wheel overhead. The waves make a gentle lapping sound as they roll on to the beach. The golden sands feel hot under your body as you relax down into them more and more.*

4. *It's breakfast time in your holiday hotel. In the background you hear the muted rattle of cutlery and crockery, and the murmur of other guests talking. Feel in your hands the sheets of the newspaper you are reading, and hear it rustle as you turn the pages. You smell the aroma of coffee in the air. You think of ordering your favourite breakfast and savour it in advance. You feel excited at the thought of the days lying ahead of you on your holiday.*

Your powers of visualisation will have enabled you to have 'seen', 'heard', 'tasted' or sensed the scenes in some way, however fleetingly. Practise with these short scenes a few times and make up some of your own.

Visualisation is a magical and stimulating skill for you to enjoy. It allows you to enter a secret world of your very own creation. In this inner world you have the opportunity to make undreamed-of changes in your life. Changes that have the potential to:

Improve your self-esteem,
Allow you to seek and find the solution to problems,
Enhance your career,
Find new ways to enjoy yourself,
Relieve all your aches and pains,
Bring healing energy to your body,
Give you succour in difficult times,
Relieve stress.

Best of all,

You will find a totally new way for peaceful sleep to
become yours every night.

Your visualisation skills are a vital element for gaining peaceful sleep at night. Much of the Peaceful Sleep Bedtime Routine which I recommend you use at bedtime is based on visualisation. Full details of the Peaceful Sleep Bedtime Routine are at the end of the book. During the visualisation you will find yourself completely immersed in timeless serenity from where you will find it truly easy to drift into a deep and peaceful sleep.

Summary

1. The techniques used in the Peaceful Sleep Bedtime Routine are of tremendous value to you to use during the day to reduce stress. The more you practise the techniques during the day, the more effective they will become when you come to use them at night.

2. Your self-talk is yours to direct. A racing mind or a barrage of negative thoughts can be stopped in its tracks with the use of the 'STOP/CANCEL/CHANGE' technique.

3. Use the power of positive affirmations to ensure that your self-talk is supportive and nurturing.

Peaceful Sleep – when I say "peaceful sleep" I fall asleep
easily and sleep right through the night

4. Repeat the Peaceful Sleep affirmation often throughout the day.

5. Initiate the 'relaxation response' by using the 'two-sighs' deep diaphragmatic breathing method.

6. Take 'breathing treat' breaks often during the day.

7. Take a full-length relaxation session every day.

8. The 'relaxation response' acts like a gateway into your inner, creative world where you can be anything and do anything you like. Take time out to practise visualising, recall events from the past in full sensual detail, or take imaginary journeys into other kingdoms.

9. Rehearse the Peaceful Sleep Bedtime Routine visualisation every day (details at the end of the book). Get to know every corner of the Secret Garden and House of Dreams that are described in the visualisation. The more you practise, the clearer and brighter the pictures in your mind will become.

10. Remember that practice is the most important element of all.

CHAPTER THREE

Making a Sleep Diary

In this chapter you will find out how to keep a sleep diary which will be of great benefit in helping you to discover the underlying cause/s of your sleeplessness. This, in turn, will help you to find ways of adjusting your lifestyle successfully in order to achieve a peaceful night's sleep every night. Spending time looking in detail at your sleep pattern and lifestyle does not mean that you are focusing on the situation in a negative way. Recording these details in diary form is a very positive move for you to take, because the more you learn and understand about your sleep pattern and your lifestyle, the easier you will find it to sleep peacefully right through the night.

On the next few pages there are sleep diaries for you to complete over the course of two weeks. The diaries consist of three simple check lists to complete each day. Each check list refers to the *previous* day and night, so be sure to complete your check lists very soon after waking up in the morning, before you become entangled in the coming day's events and distractions.

At the end of the two weeks you can analyse your diaries which will give you a far greater insight into your sleep pattern and habits. Some of the underlying reasons for your sleeplessness may become apparent, and it may then be possible to pinpoint some areas of your life where changes could be made to enhance your sleeping.

While you are completing your diaries over the two-week period, continue practising and using the techniques covered in earlier chapters. At the end of the two weeks, with this constant practice, you may well find that your sleep has already settled down to a new desirable pattern. If not, you may find it useful to continue completing the diaries to gather further information until you no longer have the challenge of poor sleep and are happy with your sleep pattern. The diaries would also make a valuable record for you to take to your GP or to a good friend if you felt you needed some further support and investigation into your sleep pattern. Familiarity with our own lifestyle means we cannot always recognise something as a potential problem area, whereas an independent eye may immediately spot something that we have overlooked.

Whatever the cause of your night-time difficulties, do not doubt that you will overcome and win through. This book is here to support you on your journey. With the powerful, transforming techniques and the soothing Peaceful Sleep Bedtime Routine in place, you will become more relaxed and confident, your life will be enhanced, as will, of course, your sleep.

Notes on Completing the Diaries

To complete your own diaries you can use the charts in the book or photocopy them if you prefer.

Each morning, very soon after waking, take a few minutes to complete the three diaries. Remember that the entry for each day refers to the *previous* twenty-four hours. If, of course, you work unusual hours, adjust the times mentioned according to your own routine.

Complete all the diaries with as much detail as you can. The more information you collect, the better placed you will be when you come to analyse your results. Feel free to enter any additional comments or items you think relevant.

Sleep Diary 1

Each morning, mark the previous night's experience as shown at the top of the chart: a tick for when you were asleep, a cross for periods of wakefulness, and a circle to represent any occasions when you got up during the night. If you fell asleep during the day, mark this also.

Sleep Diary 2

This diary is self-explanatory. It asks you to record your activities during the day and evening and also how you felt at certain times during the day, for example, whether you felt tired, alert, happy, angry, upset, or whatever.

Sleep Diary 3

Sleep Diary 3 only requires a tick for a 'Yes' response. If your answer is 'No' to any item, just leave it blank.

The check list in Sleep Diary 3 is a useful record when com-

Peaceful Sleep – when I say "peaceful sleep" I fall asleep easily and sleep right through the night

bined with the other two records because it will give you an insight into your lifestyle. You can then take all this information into account when analysing your sleep patterns. This lifestyle check list will also act as a reminder to you about the positive benefits or negative effects of certain activities.

Sleep Diary No 3 – Items of Potential Positive Benefit

Exercise in the daytime/late afternoon

Relaxation session during the day

Having a light snack at bedtime

Taking a warm bath or shower at bedtime

Keeping to regular bedtimes and wake-up times

Using the Peaceful Sleep Bedtime Routine

Having a quiet, cool and dark bedroom

Taking time to unwind and let go of the day half-an-hour before bed

Reducing stress by making a list of tasks and activities for the next day.

Clearing your mind before bedtime.

Be sure to bear the above points in mind and try to incorporate as many of them as possible into your day and evening's activities.

Sleep Diary 1

NB The diary refers to previous day/night. Complete within half an hour of waking.

✓ = Asleep,   ✗ = Not Asleep   O = Got Up

	8am	9	10	11	12	1pm	2	3	4	5	6	7	8	9	10	11	12	1am	2	3	4	5	6	7	8am
Complete on MONDAY am for previous day/night																									
Complete on TUESDAY am for previous day/night																									
Complete on WEDNESDAY am for previous day/night																									
Complete on THURSDAY am for previous day/night																									
Complete on FRIDAY am for previous day/night																									
Complete on SATURDAY am for previous day/night																									
Complete on SUNDAY am for previous day/night																									

Observations:

Sleep Diary 2

NB Refers to previous day/night. Complete within half an hour of waking

Scale: Very poor 0 .... 10 Excellent

	Hours of sleep last night	Overall quality of sleep 0-10	Main daytime activities yesterday	Main evening activities yesterday	How I felt during the day yesterday	How I felt when I went to bed last night	How I felt when I woke up this morning
Complete on MONDAY am for previous day/night							
Complete on TUESDAY am for previous day/night							
Complete on WEDNESDAY am for previous day/night							
Complete on THURSDAY am for previous day/night							
Complete on FRIDAY am for previous day/night							
Complete on SATURDAY am for previous day/night							
Complete on SUNDAY am for previous day/night							

Observations:

Sleep Diary 3

NB Refers to previous day/night. Complete within half an hour of waking.
Tick for 'Yes', leave blank for 'No'.
PSBR = Peaceful Sleep Bedtime Routine

	Mon	Tues	Wed	Thurs	Fri	Sat	Sun
POTENTIALLY BENEFICIAL ROUTINES							
Daytime Exercise							
Relaxation Session							
Snack at bedtime							
Warm bath/shower,bedtime							
Regular hour for bed							
Regular hour for waking							
Used PSBR without tape							
Used PSBR with tape							
Bedroom quiet/cool/dark							
Unwind 1/2 hour before bedtime							
Made list of tasks for next day							
POTENTIALLY NEGATIVE ROUTINES							
Nap during day							
Meal after 8.30 pm							
Caffeine after 8.30 pm							
Alcohol after 9 pm							
Smoke in evening							
Exercise in evening							
Sleeping Pills							
Other Drugs							
Herbal Remedies							
In pain/discomfort							
Any change in routine: during day							
during evening							
Any upsets in day							
Sleep quality 0-10 (as in diary 2)							
Observations							

Sleep Diary 1

NB The diary refers to previous day/night. Complete within half an hour of waking.

✓ = Asleep,   ✗ = Not Asleep   O = Got Up

	8am	9	10	11	12	1pm	2	3	4	5	6	7	8	9	10	11	12	1am	2	3	4	5	6	7	8am
Complete on MONDAY am for previous day/night																									
Complete on TUESDAY am for previous day/night																									
Complete on WEDNESDAY am for previous day/night																									
Complete on THURSDAY am for previous day/night																									
Complete on FRIDAY am for previous day/night																									
Complete on SATURDAY am for previous day/night																									
Complete on SUNDAY am for previous day/night																									

Observations:

42

Sleep Diary 2

NB Refers to previous day/night. Complete within half an hour of waking

Scale: Very poor 0 .... 10 Excellent

	Hours of sleep last night	Overall quality of sleep 0-10	Main daytime activities yesterday	Main evening activities yesterday	How I felt during the day yesterday	How I felt when I went to bed last night	How I felt when I woke up this morning
Complete on MONDAY am for previous day/night							
Complete on TUESDAY am for previous day/night							
Complete on WEDNESDAY am for previous day/night							
Complete on THURSDAY am for previous day/night							
Complete on FRIDAY am for previous day/night							
Complete on SATURDAY am for previous day/night							
Complete on SUNDAY am for previous day/night							

Observations:

Sleep Diary 3

NB Refers to previous day/night. Complete within half an hour of waking.
Tick for 'Yes', leave blank for 'No'.
PSBR = Peaceful Sleep Bedtime Routine

	Mon	Tues	Wed	Thurs	Fri	Sat	Sun
POTENTIALLY BENEFICIAL ROUTINES							
Daytime Exercise							
Relaxation Session							
Snack at bedtime							
Warm bath/shower,bedtime							
Regular hour for bed							
Regular hour for waking							
Used PSBR without tape							
Used PSBR with tape							
Bedroom quiet/cool/dark							
Unwind 1/2 hour before bedtime							
Made list of tasks for next day							
POTENTIALLY NEGATIVE ROUTINES							
Nap during day							
Meal after 8.30 pm							
Caffeine after 8.30 pm							
Alcohol after 9 pm							
Smoke in evening							
Exercise in evening							
Sleeping Pills							
Other Drugs							
Herbal Remedies							
In pain/discomfort							
Any change in routine: during day							
during evening							
Any upsets in day							
Sleep quality 0-10 (as in diary 2)							
Observations							

How to Analyse Your Diaries

When you have completed your two weeks of information gathering, take some time when you can be undisturbed to look quietly at your diaries. Bring to the diaries the impartial attitude of a scientist who is analytically searching for conclusions. Distance yourself from the process a little in order to keep a positive, rational and constructive attitude. This is not an opportunity to be critical of yourself and, even if your sleep pattern is still poor, remember that this exercise is being done with the sole aim of overcoming the challenge of disturbed and restless sleep. So, be kind to yourself and let go any negative thoughts about your sleep that may come to your mind. Say to yourself, with real feeling,

"I am calm and confident, I am totally adequate at all times, I am strong and capable and I am overcoming a challenge in my life right now."

When doing your investigations, take into account that there may be more than one reason for poor quality sleep.

Sleep Diary 1

First of all, take a look at the pattern of your sleep in Sleep Diary 1. There are four basic sleep patterns into which most poor sleepers fall. See if your sleep falls into one or more of these categories.

1. *Difficulty in getting off to sleep – where it takes more than fifteen minutes or so to fall asleep.*

2. *Long periods of wakefulness during the night.*

3. *Interrupted short periods of sleep throughout the night.*

4. *Waking early and being unable to return to sleep.*

Peaceful Sleep – when I say "peaceful sleep" I fall asleep easily and sleep right through the night

You may feel you don't fit any of the above categories – even sleep professionals have no definitive answers to the questions of why people don't sleep and why they wake up at certain times. If so, don't let it be a source of concern, continue with analysing Diaries 2 and 3, and concentrate on the techniques of the Peaceful Sleep Bedtime Routine and the additional ideas in this book which will help you to win through in your search for peaceful sleep.

Category 1 – Difficulty with Falling Asleep

If you have difficulty in falling asleep when you first go to bed, it is very likely that your mind is still busy with events from the day or your body is buzzing with adrenaline from some sort of over-stimulation in the evening. Almost any factor in your life could be the cause of this and you will probably find what it is with careful investigation of Sleep Diaries 2 and 3. Remember, whatever the cause of the difficulty in falling asleep the answer is the relaxing Peaceful Sleep Bedtime Routine which you can use over and over as many times as necessary until you float into a peaceful sleep. You may also like to add some comforting affirmations. Try some of those in the next section, Category 2. If sleep still eludes you, don't lie tossing and turning, get up and do something relaxing, read your Action Plan for Peaceful Sleep (see p. 00) or listen to some music. Return to bed when you feel sleepy and repeat the Peaceful Sleep Bedtime Routine.

Categories 2 and 3 – Waking in the Night

The cause of waking in the night, as with difficulty with falling asleep when you first go to bed, can be from almost any element in your life that troubles you, plus being woken up from disturbing dreams or drinking alcohol. Although there can be many reasons for waking during the night, often the trigger is not having let go of the previous day's concerns. If you tend to wake up with your mind churning round and round, tackle it with the 'STOP' technique followed by a positive affirmation.

Either out aloud or inside your head, say to yourself a firm

"STOP!" or *"STOP THAT!"*

and you will gain a moment of surprised silence in your mind. Then quickly fill the space you've made for yourself by saying,

*"I let go of those thoughts. **Tomorrow** is for thinking, **NOW** is for relaxing."*

and, if the thoughts you have are negative or anxious,

"I focus on the good things of today. More good things will happen tomorrow."

Then go through all the good things that happened to you the previous day, sift through the day's events and collect all the tiny nuggets of gold. It doesn't matter how small they were – for example, a smile from someone, a compliment at work, the way the sun shone through the trees, your cat purring. Concentrate on these aspects of your life to lead your thoughts away from those that may be troublesome.

Challenging situations from the day can affect your sleep. If there is something specific worrying you, write it on a piece of paper, place the paper in a drawer and shut it firmly away. When you shut the drawer say to yourself,

*"I will think about that **tomorrow**."*

We always sleep far more than we may realise. It doesn't help to count the hours you *think* you have been asleep or awake. So, no more clock-watching! Cover or turn your clock so you can't see the time, say, *"STOP!"* to those negative thoughts about time passing and follow it by telling yourself,

Peaceful Sleep – when I say "peaceful sleep" I fall asleep easily and sleep right through the night

"Time doesn't matter. My mind and my body are resting peacefully."

After any of these affirmations, continue with the Peaceful Sleep Bedtime Routine and you will soon be deeply asleep again.

Category 4 – Early Waking

If you wake early in the morning and seem unable to return to sleep, this can sometimes be because of the effects of alcohol or sleeping pills taken the previous evening. If you think this may possibly be your concern, you may have to consider your position regarding them and reflect upon weaning yourself from them. If you need support or guidance, you could discuss the situation with a health professional or seek advice from one of the addresses at the end of the book. Advice on coming off sleeping pills is also in Chapter 5.

Early waking can also be a sign of anxiety or depression. If you think this is relevant to you, make a plan to tackle it, using relaxation and other strategies from this book. If you feel really 'stuck' with an emotion, consider asking for professional help for a while.

Meanwhile, if you are awake in bed, use the time in a positive way. Quiet relaxation is of great benefit and you may find that sleep creeps up on you unnoticed. Go through the Peaceful Sleep Body Scan again and again. While you are relaxing, your body will benefit from resting quietly and will begin its restoration process. Remember the three Rs, and say to yourself,

"Time doesn't matter. As I Relax and Rest, my body is being Restored."

Sleep Diaries 2 and 3

After investigating the pattern of your sleep, take a careful look at the first eleven items of Sleep Diary 3, the Potentially Beneficial Routines. Are you regularly placing a tick beside most of these items? If not, do consider introducing more of them into your lifestyle as all of these items are potentially of great support to you and make a positive contribution towards gaining peaceful sleep.

Now, take a very close look at the last items on the check list of Sleep Diary 3, the Potentially Negative Routines. Are you regularly placing a tick against many of these items? This part of the check list, plus your responses to the questions about your activities and feelings in Sleep Diary 3, are where you will be most likely to find the root cause/s of your disturbed sleep.

The headings on the check list in Sleep Diaries 2 and 3 are mostly self-explanatory but a little more information about some of the entries may be useful to you:

Your Daytime and Evening Activities

Scrutinise your activities and routines during the day and evening and consider whether they are affecting your sleep in any way. Perhaps a sleepless night tends to follow a particular activity? If so, consider why this could be and ask yourself if there is any action you could take. Perhaps over-stimulation in the day or evening is followed by a broken night's sleep? If this happens to you, it's because the adrenaline from over-excitement inhibits sleep and, when it's still flowing at night, instead of being able to relax, you end up with a whirling mind and a restless, uncomfortable night. So, if this is a your sleep pattern, it's best to avoid horror movies, intense conversations, heated discussions, or whatever else caused the over-stimulation, and to spend extra time with calming, relaxing activities, including the addition of further relaxation sessions.

Your Feelings – Physical and Emotional

We are not well-placed to sleep easily and peacefully at night if we go to bed in a highly-charged emotional state with adrenaline

Peaceful Sleep – when I say "peaceful sleep" I fall asleep easily and sleep right through the night

rushing around our bodies, our minds overactive and our feelings raw. How we feel physically is often a result of how we feel emotionally. The two are strongly linked and many of the difficulties around sleep are caused by challenges from the day which often have an emotional content and have not been addressed or resolved. These emotional disturbances can be from anything at all in your life, from family strains to worries about financial or work-related problems.

Check with Sleep Diaries 2 and 3 to see how you were feeling, both physically and emotionally, at various times of the day. Do you tend to find yourself feeling a particular emotion or physical state very often at either bedtime or in the morning? For example, do you feel anxious and wide awake at bedtime? How do you feel in the mornings? Do you feel depressed with no enthusiasm for the day ahead? Or do you feel alert and keen to start the day? Is the emotion all of a similar type, stemming from similar situations? Do disturbed emotional feelings affect your sleep? Is there any pattern here that you can observe?

Any emotional distress, whether coming from your response to a situation or from your inner feelings, can sow the seeds for disturbed sleep. When we are in an emotional turmoil of some kind, rational, constructive thoughts are not available to us. We all have negative feelings some of the time, this is perfectly normal. However we need to remember that we are responsible for our own feelings. We make *ourselves* angry, irritable anxious or upset by our response to the other person or situation. In other words, we upset *ourselves*. By realising that you upset yourself and *you* are responsible for the way you feel, and it is *not* someone else's fault, you become more in control of the situation and can work on handling your own emotions. You cannot change other people and the way they think or act, you can only change yourself.

While it is normal to feel negative emotions – and no emotions are, in themselves, 'good' or 'bad' – there are certainly inappropriate ways to *express* those feelings. For example, instead of harbouring resentment, anger or anxiety and going to bed filled with those feelings, it is far better to acknowledge and tackle them, perhaps through talking about them or writing them out. This will go some way towards dispelling the emotions and to tackling the cause of the difficulty. Again, the 'STOP' technique is useful in handling the escalation of emotion. Say *"STOP"* firmly to yourself and then follow it with,

"I am calm. I am taking a step back from this situation. I am now thinking rationally about what to do next."

Another source of poor sleep to be considered is a possible underlying discontent with your lifestyle as it is at the moment. If your needs and wants in life are not being fulfilled, your inner self will be restless and will try to make itself heard at night when you are quiet and not distracted by events of the day. If this rings true for you, take time out to use the exercise in Chapter 4 to find out what your needs and wants are.

Sometimes long-term sleeplessness can be the result of a short-term stressful event which initially caused a few nights of poor sleep. It is possible for a few sleep-disturbed nights to trigger a downward spiral of anxiety and negative thinking about sleeping which may lead to yet more poor sleep. As this pattern of poor sleep develops, the original cause might even be forgotten. Then anxiety about sleeping itself becomes the main concern, rather than the cause of the insomnia. So a cycle is set up of poor sleep/worry about sleep/poor sleep ... and so on. If this has happened to you, you can break this cycle by concentrating on working on positive thinking, relaxation and other techniques in this book.

Bereavement and any other deeply upsetting life event, such as an accident or childhood trauma, can often show itself in later

Peaceful Sleep – when I say "peaceful sleep" I fall asleep easily and sleep right through the night

life. Don't hesitate to seek advice from a health professional if you have any long-term unresolved anxiety or depression.

Exercise

Exercise, or the lack of it, can be the cause of being unable to sleep. Too little exercise may mean you are not physically tired enough to fall asleep. On the other hand, exercising late in the evening increases your chances of staying awake! This is because adrenaline is produced by exercise and adrenaline production inhibits sleep. However, twenty minutes or so of exercise in the late afternoon, preferably in fresh air, can be very beneficial in helping you to sleep more easily. So, think carefully before you go for any kind of evening exercise session if you think it will affect your sleep later that night.

Eating, Drinking and Smoking in the Evening

Sleep difficulties can arise from elements of food and drink consumption – both *when* you eat and *what* you eat. For example, eating chocolate or drinking coffee, tea or cola – all of which contain the stimulant caffeine – in the evening can mean disturbed, wakeful nights. Having a meal late in the evening can also keep your digestive system active – and you awake. Another cause of poor sleep, particularly if you are anorexic, is not having enough to eat. If you think food may be behind your sleep difficulty, try altering your eating habits until you find your sleep improves. A traditional aid for peaceful sleep is a warm milky drink at bedtime with a small sustaining snack, such as crackers or a piece of toast.

Many people have alcohol at night in an attempt to help them sleep but, although they may drop off to sleep quickly, disturbed sleep and early wakening is usually the result of drinking at night. Unfortunately, when a sleepless person has a drink the effect is multiplied, so one glass of wine can become the equivalent of many more. Smoking or a smoky atmosphere can also contribute to restless sleep. If either smoking or drinking are ticked on your list and are affecting your sleep, the answer is in your hands, although you may need some support in giving up or cutting down if either smoking or drinking is a long-term habit.

Sleeping Pills, Other Drugs, Herbal Remedies

It is possible that some prescription drugs can disturb your sleep pattern, so check to see if your insomnia has worsened since starting a particular course of drugs. Sleeping pills and herbal remedies can be useful in the short-term to help you over a brief crisis. If you need the assistance of a herb or a pill occasionally, that's fine, but, as we all know, it is far better not to have to rely on pills or herbs at all. Sleeping pills can cause many other problems and are notoriously difficult to withdraw from or reduce. Stopping sleeping pills needs a properly organised campaign of action so that you don't suffer withdrawal symptoms. Please see Chapter 5 if you wish to do this. It's also important to avoid over-the-counter remedies, as they may prove to be psychologically addictive and may interfere with your normal sleep pattern.

Pain/Discomfort/Medical Problems

Many medical problems can affect your sleep, especially conditions which produce pain or the need to go to the bathroom during the night. If you share your bedroom, ask your partner to tell you about any particularly odd movements or behaviour, unusual snoring and breathing noises. If there is anything unusual to report about your sleep it would be advisable to have it checked medically.

If you do have any medical problems try to get the basic condition under control. If the condition persists, tackle the sleep situation with an even greater input of relaxation and other techniques from the Peaceful Sleep Routine. Concentrate on the

Peaceful Sleep – when I say "peaceful sleep" I fall asleep easily and sleep right through the night

healing input achieved from stilling your mind, remaining calm and positive and using deep diaphragmatic breathing and relaxation methods to release those healthy 'feelgood' endorphins.

Bedroom Ambience

Is it possible that there is something in your surroundings that is contributing to poor sleep? Perhaps you are being disturbed by noise from outside your bedroom? Or perhaps your bedroom is not dark or cool enough to encourage deep sleep? Perhaps you have an old or uncomfortable bed? These points can be taken care of reasonably easily once they are recognised. It is very important to keep your bedroom for sleep only. If your bedroom is used as an office, for eating, drinking, watching TV or other activities that normally take place elsewhere, the message is not given to your subconscious mind that this is the place for sleeping.

If you experience interrupted short periods of sleep, it is possible that this is caused by noise of some kind. Solving this might be easily accomplished with double glazing and/or earplugs, though a better solution in the long term would be to learn techniques which will train your brain to ignore and accept the noise. This can be done with a simple meditation practice in which you develop an attitude of not minding the noise, just accepting it as it is as nothing to concern you. Let the noise flow past you instead of getting hooked up into it. Another mental strategy is to turn the noise around so that you perceive it as a good sound. You can invent a story around it. Perhaps, if it's traffic noise, you can elaborate to yourself on a story about, say, people going the holiday of a lifetime as a treat for their children.

Regular Hours

Irregular bedtimes can be a big contributor to a poor night's sleep. Our inner rhythms are regulated by the increase and decrease in production of hormones in our brains. Our internal systems are built to function at different levels for the day and night with different chemicals being released in our bodies. When our 'body' or 'biological' clock is disturbed by late nights, irregular bedtimes, shift work or air travel, it interferes with our chemical balance, making us feel tired with low energy levels.

Dr. John Taub of Charlottesville, Virginia, undertook a study which compared a group of people who kept regular hours to a group whose hours of bedtime varied. He found that those who kept regular hours had faster reaction times and felt happier and more energetic than those who were irregular in their sleeping habits. The 'irregular' group also became less efficient and had less of a sense of wellbeing. This is because regular hours also help to keep the sleep and wakefulness hormones operating in harmony.

You can strengthen your 'biological clock' very easily by keeping regular hours for bedtime and waking up in the morning. If you have been keeping irregular hours try sticking to the same bedtime for two or three weeks to strengthen you body's internal clock- and don't be tempted to have 'lie-ins' or naps unless absolutely unavoidable. The time we feel sleepy at night is governed by the time we get up in the morning. If you find it difficult to go to sleep try fooling your body rhythms in this way:

Get up fifteen minutes earlier each day and keep to the same bedtime in the evening. Do this for a week or two in order to 'reset' your biological clock. If you still don't drop off to sleep easily, try getting up another fifteen minutes earlier for a further week or so. Continue like this, gradually rising earlier by ten or fifteen minutes every few weeks until you reach a time where you fall asleep with ease at night. This plan will encourage your inner clock to follow a new pattern until you find the optimum bedtime.

Peaceful Sleep – when I say "peaceful sleep" I fall asleep easily and sleep right through the night

Conclusion

Now that you have analysed your Sleep Diaries you may well have been able to identify the cause of your sleep difficulties. Do you think your poor sleep is linked to a particular stress in your life at the moment, and is this likely to ease? Is there something particular in your sleep behaviour which you could change? If you have found a likely cause, work out a plan of action to deal with it. At the same time, continue practising and using the whole armoury of techniques you have learned, and you will soon win through and achieve your goal of peaceful sleep at night.

If you have not yet discovered the cause of your sleepless-ness, continue to keep your diaries until you do. Meanwhile, continue supporting and nourishing yourself by practising and using all the Peaceful Sleep techniques. Remember, we all have the odd period of disturbed sleep and hardly anyone has unbroken sleep. As we get older, we tend to wake up on more occasions during the night. The attitude to take here is, again, one of not minding being woken up, such as,

"Ah well........ I'll just go through my lovely Peaceful Sleep visualisation again and I'll soon be back asleep."

Continue using all the techniques and the Peaceful Sleep Bedtime Routine until you are able to cope well with your work, feel reasonably alert during the day, enjoy life and no longer regard your sleep as an area of anxiety or concern.

CHAPTER FOUR

Techniques to Enrich Your Life

With the mind-body techniques in this chapter you can change the way you feel and act. You don't *have* to feel stressed, anxious, irritable or any other negative emotion. It is within your own power to change to more positive feelings and behaviour. It is unavoidable and perfectly normal to have stresses and strains in your life. Provided you know how to handle them, and not be led by them, *you* will be in charge of your life. The very fact and feeling of being in charge of your own life, shaping its pattern and form, will be sufficient to overcome the negative effects of stress, and your sleep will, as a result, be more peaceful and healing.

There are some very simple ways in which you can enrich your life and, in so doing, increase your sleep potential. As you know, when your life is balanced and harmonious sleep comes easily, as to a child. When your inner self is at peace and happy with the way you are, it has no need to disturb your nights in an attempt to receive some attention for its needs and wants. The additional techniques in this chapter will help to ensure your sleep by increasing the nurturing, self-loving time you spend during the day. With the techniques in this chapter you can learn how to use your time wisely, how to foster a positive attitude, how to solve problems and protect yourself from negative influences, how to use the practice of meditation to overcome stress and how to discover your deepest needs and wants in life and ensure that they are being met. By developing a supporting, caring attitude to yourself, the whole quality of your life will improve. You will be rewarded with a balanced life, full of wellbeing, vitality – and peaceful sleep at night.

The technique that follows can be used to systematically build your sense of personal value and self-confidence and can also act directly on the way you approach your sleep. As your own positivity increases, it will bring a more relaxed approach to life and, of course, will reduce stress, thus again improving the quality of your sleep.

As you know, the thoughts you think have a direct influence on the way you feel and act. The reverse is also true. **The way you use your body influences your thoughts and feelings.** Try this quick experiment for yourself:

Take a moment to notice how you are feeling right now. Make a mental note of your feelings and your thoughts.

Now let your body sag, your head droop down, put the fingers of one hand near your mouth, gaze down at the ground.

Notice how you are feeling now. Do you feel differently from how you felt before you started?

And now,

Look up to the sky, stretch your arms wide as though embracing nature, the sun and the fresh air, relax your features and smile.

How do you feel now?

Do you feel differently from how you felt in the first posture?

You were only acting but I feel sure your thoughts and feelings changed quite perceptibly with each body posture. No doubt as a result of your body language in the first experiment, you momentarily felt more downbeat and negative, even though it was not necessarily true of you at the time. In the second experiment I expect you felt your feelings change briefly to those of openness and of being uplifted.

What actually happens is that your subconscious mind is open to information from both your thoughts and from your body. Now, if your body language is such that it signifies, say, elation, your subconscious mind registers that message and so reflects that emotion in your feelings. The stronger you make the body language message, the stronger the feelings will become. If you add some relevant positive thoughts in the form of affirmations, the message to your subconscious mind is made even louder and clearer.

This technique can truly empower you, giving you confidence and strength in many situations, particularly in the area of your sleep. Imagine the *power* of this technique and the positive changes you can make in your life. When you use this technique, although you may be acting or pretending to be something you are not currently feeling or thinking, you are *not* deceiving yourself, you are giving yourself instructions or directions as to how you would *like* to be. *You* are in charge, and you are consciously using and taking advantage of the

Peaceful Sleep – when I say "peaceful sleep" I fall asleep easily and sleep right through the night

way your mind works in order to bring about changes that you desire. So, by acting as though you are, for instance, a person who is calm and confident, the feelings will follow; you will become and feel calmer and more confident. By acting in your life as though you are a positive, resourceful person, you will gradually become that positive, resourceful person.

The technique uses a simple question format to bring about the changes you want. By asking yourself questions your subconscious mind will automatically produce answers for you. The question to ask yourself is:

"How would it be if I was ....(e.g. calm and confident)............?"

You can add to this effect by *acting* as though you are already that person and have already achieved your goal. Try this technique out in relation to your sleep. The question to ask yourself in relation to your sleep is:

"How would it be if I was a person who slept peacefully all night?"

Before you try it out, practise the question in the following way, using a short breath-awareness and relaxation technique to lead you into the question.

Act and Be

Take a few minutes or so to sit or lie down quietly where you won't be disturbed. Become aware of your breathing and notice the gentle rise and fall of your body as you breathe in and out. On your next out-breath, let your breath out through your mouth with a slight sigh.

On the next out-breath, imagine the sigh going down from the top of your head to the soles of your feet. As you let all the air go, feel the tension drain away. Now just breathe normally through your nose and think of yourself as being in a typical day of yours......................

and then ask yourself,

"How would it be if I was a person who slept peacefully all night?"

...................and imagine yourself acting as if you were a person who did sleep peacefully all night. Watch yourself as you go through your day in this new mode, the mode of a person who sleeps peacefully all night long, without anxiety about sleeping. Imagine the different way you would handle your day if you had a good night's sleep every night. Imagine how you would be when you are getting up, while you are preparing breakfast, in any work you do, in your social activities and in your personal life. Take yourself through your day, but only up to the early evening.

To help you with the picture, ask yourself some questions, such as,

"How would I go about my day?"

"What would I be feeling?"

"How would I look?"

"How would I be moving?"

"What would I do?"

Now, imagine yourself at bedtime, and ask yourself the same initial question again,

"How would it be if I was a person who slept peacefully all night?"

Imagine yourself acting as if you were a person who slept peacefully all night and see how you would behave at bedtime. Watch yourself as you go through your bedtime preparations and settle down in bed in the mode of a person who sleeps peacefully all night long.................... See yourself calm and relaxed, perhaps enjoying a milky drink, going through your bathroom routine, possibly having a luxurious scented bath, settling down in bed, resting your head on the pillow and allowing sleep to come to you...............

Peaceful Sleep – when I say "peaceful sleep" I fall asleep easily and sleep right through the night

To help you with the picture, ask yourself some questions, such as,

"What would I be feeling?"
"How would I look?"
"How would I be moving?"
"What would I be thinking?"

And now gradually return your awareness to the room, feeling relaxed, confident and positive, knowing that you can actually recreate the way you felt in the visualisation at any time during the day and at bedtime when you act as though you are indeed a person who sleeps peacefully right through the night, every night.

As you go through this exercise you will find, by acting as though you are a person who sleeps peacefully, that you will become endowed with the qualities of someone who sleeps well. This has been achieved in your imagination, but having experienced the feeling inside yourself, you have given yourself the power to be able to carry the actions through in real life. And so, take time during the day to ask yourself the question, "How would it be if I was a person who slept peacefully all night?" and allow yourself to actually *be* that person. At night, do the same, allow your inner self to take care of you in the way it knows best and you will soon find yourself sinking down into a deep peaceful sleep.

Once you are familiar with the technique you can use it at any time when you find yourself feeling in a negative frame of mind. Choose qualities that are relevant to you and ask yourself,

"How would it be if I was a ....(insert desired quality here)................person?"

Your wise inner self knows the answer and, by asking, you release the inner power to act in that way.

To add to the positive effect of this technique, question yourself further as you did in the previous exercise. The answers will help you achieve your desired result. Take notice of any answers you receive, no matter how brief or unusual. It is important to find a positive way to handle some of the answers that may have come to your mind. For example, if you asked, 'How would it be if I was a fit and healthy person?' and your inner self gave you the answer that you need to go on a diet or stop smoking, you would need to find a positive way to accept this answer in order to carry it out. We may not always want, or find it easy, to do the things we know would be of benefit to us!

This exercise is an important and creative addition to your storehouse of supportive techniques. It has the potential to transform your whole way of being.

Meditation

We cope better in life if we accept and deal with what is happening *now*, in the present moment, and let the future take care of itself. Coming into the present moment on a regular basis is an unusual experience for most of us, as we tend to go through our days on 'automatic pilot', lost in our thoughts, which are often worry-thoughts. When we come to the end of a day we will probably have spent much of it in a half-awake daze, missing all the small yet wonderful happenings around us in the natural world. These precious moments enrich us and balance the frenetic activity of our busy lives.

Through the practice of meditation we can spend more and more of our time mindfully in the present. A side effect of meditation is that it allows the relaxation response and the production of endorphins to be kindled. Endorphins, as you will remember, are our body's own 'feelgood', relaxing chemicals. They have the opposite effect in our bodies to that pro-

Peaceful Sleep – when I say "peaceful sleep" I fall asleep easily and sleep right through the night

duced by the chemicals in the 'flight or fight' stress response, which only serve to agitate and frighten us.

The practice of meditation will also allow us to become aware of our mind, how it functions, and how our attitudes and thoughts lead us either to the stress response or away from it into peace. With the practice of meditation we learn to accept and let go of negative, uncomfortable thoughts and feelings. Meditating also allows our inner wisdom to surface more often; we enable our wise inner self to show us how to make the wisest choices in life and how best to live our lives. The practice of meditation can be exceptionally powerful in the domain of sleep and coping with agitated thoughts at night. And so you can see, it is a useful skill for you to have in addition to the other techniques. In fact, the practice of meditation can have such far-reaching effects that many people eventually choose to use meditation alone of all the techniques as it satisfies their deepest needs.

You may not realise it, but you may be taking part in a meditation when you are gardening, cooking, sewing, rubbing down wood or, indeed, taking part in any other activity that keeps your attention firmly rooted in the present moment. On these occasions, your mind isn't wandering off with thoughts of the past, the future, planning what to say in a meeting or what to have for dinner.

To meditate successfully all you need to do is to make some time to actually *meditate*. There is no such thing as a 'successful' meditation or an 'unsuccessful' meditation, all that matters is that you *do it*. That is, you spend between ten and twenty minutes once, preferably twice, a day just sitting in silence. All that is required is that you watch your breath as it flows in and out, or watch your thoughts and feelings as they come and go. Have an attitude of not minding if the thoughts or emotions are turbulent or peaceful. Just let the thoughts or emotions pass you by and accept things as they are, without trying to change anything in any way. When we meditate mindfully and cease to be judgmental about ourselves or anything outside ourselves, we leave behind the everyday world and go to a quiet centre within where there is only and always peace and stillness.

When you sit still and just watch your mind, you notice that a huge and never-ending jumble of thoughts and sensations are produced. So as not to get hooked into these thoughts, most people like to have a focus of some kind for their mind. The focus can be anything at all from a word or phrase to a candle or even your own thumbnail, but a most useful focus is your breath which is always there and available to you, especially at night when you are in bed.

Bring that attitude of 'not minding' to your meditation, that attitude of acceptance and 'letting go' to whatever comes into your awareness. By letting go of thoughts and sensations as they arise, you will allow them to pass without affecting you, to rise and fall, rather like the waves in the sea on the surface of your mind. No matter how tumultuous the thoughts or sensations may be at times, they will float away from you, and 'the sea', or your mind, will become a calmer more peaceful place.

Basic Mindfulness Meditation

Sit in a quiet, comfortable place where you can be undisturbed for ten to twenty minutes. There is no need to sit in any special way unless you want to use a traditional yoga-type meditation posture. If you choose to lie down be aware that you might fall asleep. To help you to remain alert, sit as straight as you can without causing any extra muscular tension. Sitting in a chair, make sure your feet are flat on the ground, your clothes are loose around your abdomen and that you have removed your glasses or any jewellery that you think might be a distraction.

Close your eyes, take your attention to your abdomen and just notice the rise and fall of your breath as it enters and leaves your body. Don't try to alter it in any way.

Peaceful Sleep – when I say "peaceful sleep" I fall asleep easily and sleep right through the night

Now take your mind around your body and relax and let go of each part in turn, starting with your feet and moving up through your body to finish with your head and face.

Now, breathing through your nose, just sit and observe your breath as it enters and leaves your body. Don't try to alter it in any way, just follow it as it flows in and out in its own time. If you wish to use a word as a focus instead of your breath, say your chosen word on the out-breath. Your word may be something like 'peace', 'love', even just the word 'one' or some other word that has no particular meaning attached to it for you.

From time to time your thoughts will wander. When you notice this happening, just note the thoughts and, without judging yourself or getting impatient, let them go. If you have worry thoughts about how you are doing, let these go too; then gently bring your attention back to your breath again. It doesn't matter how many times you have to do this, all that matters is that you are sitting in stillness for the length of time you have decided upon.

Continue in this way throughout the meditation, becoming aware when you are not with your breath or your word, then gently returning your attention to it. You can check the time every now and then if you want to and, when the time is up, open your eyes and sit quietly for a short while, enjoying the feelings you have created. Take these peaceful, calm feelings with you as you gently recommence activity.

Remember there is no such thing as a 'good' meditation or a 'bad' meditation, it's just a meditation. The process is what counts, actually sitting down and going through the practice of meditation for the set time. It doesn't matter how many times you have to bring yourself back to your chosen focus. The 'wandering mind' effect is the same for everyone, no matter how long they have been practising meditation. Return to your focus as many times as is necessary, without fighting, analysing or struggling with the thoughts. Just observe them, let them go, and then go back to your breath or your word. You may have to do this twenty, fifty or a hundred times, it doesn't matter. You aren't trying to be anything or get anywhere, you are just allowing yourself to be whatever you are in that moment, and from moment to moment. You are merely being alert and aware and fully conscious in each moment. As you progress, you will find that your levels of attention and concentration will improve and your mind will become peaceful. Before long, the benefits you gain will overflow into your whole daily life, and that centre of calmness will remain with you, even in the midst of the most difficult situations.

Sleep and Meditation

As soon as you lie down and shut your eyes, your body is conditioned to go to sleep, which is why you may fall asleep during a meditation session spent lying down. This makes meditation an appropriate routine at or before bedtime. To go to sleep you *have* to let go, you cannot force sleep to come. Sleep can only come when you let go of aroused thoughts, whether the arousal is from enjoyment or from anxiety, which is why mindfulness meditation is perfect in this situation. Many people also choose to meditate if they have disturbed sleep and find themselves awake in the night. The sleep that has been lost in this way can be recovered by the processes that take place in your body during meditation. However, don't let your only use of meditation be at bedtime or in the middle of a restless night; that's not the time to practise a new skill. You need to practise during the day when you are awake and alert and can gain experience of letting your thoughts pass by in a dispassionate way, without their affecting you. So, use your bedtime meditation session not for practice but to quieten your mind and to allow yourself to drift into sleep.

Peaceful Sleep – when I say "peaceful sleep" I fall asleep easily and sleep right through the night

How to Meditate When Wakeful at Night

When you notice that your thoughts are churning around and around, one way of dealing with the situation is to bring your awareness to your breath, and to do this over and over again, as many times as it takes. If you have discomfort somewhere in your body, you can handle it in the same way, returning to your breath instead of dwelling on the pain. Anchor your mind in your breath and say "STOP" to thinking. Just 'be': be in your breath and in the present moment. There should be no sense of ignoring or fighting the pain or thoughts. Just have an attitude of not minding, an acceptance that they are there, part of your current experience. Adopting this attitude will allow the pain or thoughts to drift away, and you to become calmer and relaxed.

Fighting, suppressing and resisting physical sensations increase anxiety, pain and the stress response. Letting go into the sensations encourages the relaxation response, gives relief from pain – and fosters sleep. Another excellent way to deal with pain is to take the opposite path, to go right into any discomfort and experience it totally, just feeling. *You will find the sensation changes and eventually subsides. You can take each breath right into the pain and breathe the pain out on the outbreath. Once the label of 'pain' is removed, the discomfort becomes only a sensation of some kind. This makes it easier to accept and, consequently, more likely to dissipate and ease.*

You can handle uncomfortable thoughts in a similar way. Breathe into them and watch them as they come and go. Anxious thoughts will seem less powerful and threatening if you can see them as just thoughts and not as your reality or as the truth. See the thoughts come and let them go, see them come and let them go, over and over again. You will come to understand that thoughts do come and go and are not the truth but are the product of an agitated mind. Just because you think a thought it does not mean that what you think will happen, or that the thought is a fact or reality. Thoughts are just thoughts and have no power over you. 'You', the real you, are the power behind the thoughts and you can choose to let them go and for them not to affect you. So continue to watch the thoughts come and watch them go, as they will.

At first, practise this type of meditation during the day at a time when you are not particularly stressed. Later on, of course, you can use it to great effect at any time during the day or night. You will find that you will be able to deal with any problems or challenges in a far more clear-minded way.

Success cannot fail to come when you practise meditation. This is because the only thing that matters is that you are willing to go through the process of looking at your mind and being with your thoughts – whether they are disturbed or otherwise – as they come. You are not aiming to get anywhere or do anything other than to be aware, to 'be', to be awake to the current moment. This is the reason meditation is so therapeutic and beneficial, and this is the way you will gain peace in your body and your mind. Nurture yourself with the practice of 'mindfulness' meditation, and new understanding and changes of attitude will continue to delight and please you on your journey through life.

What Do You Want in Life?

Many of us feel, at a deep level, that we are dissatisfied with our lives in some way but can't quite put our finger on exactly what it is that makes us feel unfulfilled. With this technique you can identify your most important wants and needs and so begin the process of expanding your life to include those things that will give enrichment and satisfaction. There is an inner, intuitive, part of you that knows instinctively what you want and need. This technique allows you to get in touch with

Peaceful Sleep – when I say "peaceful sleep" I fall asleep easily and sleep right through the night

that part to find your answers. Everyone can do this; all you need is to be open to the technique and to listen quietly to the messages from your inner self.

You will need some sheets of plain A4 paper and a pen or pencil and to be undisturbed for a short while in a quiet and comfortable place.

Getting in Touch with Your Inner Wisdom

Before you begin, relax a little by becoming aware of your breathing and allowing it to become a little deeper and slower for a few moments. Now, as you breathe out, relax your face and allow a gentle smile to play around your mouth. This will ensure that you are relaxed and in a contemplative mood.

Quietly pick up your pen or pencil, let yourself relax a little more and write "What do I want?" at the top of the page.

*Take note of the very first thought or answer that comes to your mind. This is your inner wisdom, your intuition, speaking. Write the response under the question. There's no need to try or to force answers to come. This intuitive part of you will always know what it is you truly need and desire. If nothing comes, relax again, continue to breathe quietly for a few moments more and then ask the question again. Let your imagination run free, don't censor anything. Whatever comes to your mind, however outrageous or seemingly impossible to achieve, write it down. You are going to find out what you **really** want in your life. There's no-one to impress or to please, this exercise is just for you, and it's for your eyes only. So open up and admit your long-held desires and dreams, no matter whether they are 'ordinary' or more ambitious or far-fetched. And now ask yourself,*

"What else do I want?"

and again write down the answer. Keep asking 'What else do I want?' until you have exhausted all possibilities. Fill at least one side of the paper.

Next, write at the top of another sheet of paper,

"*What do I need?*"

Relax and allow your mind spontaneously to produce answers for you. Write them down under the heading. Relax again, and then ask,

"*What else do I need?*"

Once more, allow answers to surface by themselves. Write them down as they arrive and ask the question of yourself over and over until you have exhausted all possible responses. Take as much time as you need for this.

When you have finished, sit back and look at your two lists and notice the differences between them. Notice the way in which your wants may be different from your needs. You may find this most illuminating. (If you are only reading this exercise, please go back and actually do it now, any difference in the answers can only be appreciated by going through the exercise.) Your desires may not be 'things' like 'a better car', but more elusive qualities, such as 'happiness' or 'more confidence'.

Think carefully about how you will achieve what you need and want from life. Look at your lists and find out which items have the greatest appeal to you, the biggest charge for you, and number them in order of importance. Make these top few items your immediate goals. You can work on the others later on, although you may notice that they have arrived unbidden whilst you are working on your main goals.

Ask yourself other questions to find out how to achieve your goals, desires and needs. Ask pertinent questions such as, "What do I need to do to achieve this?", "What is the first thing I need to do?" and "Are any of my desires in conflict with each other?" If one desire is in conflict with another, sometimes sacri-

Peaceful Sleep – when I say "peaceful sleep" I fall asleep easily and sleep right through the night

fices may have to be made in order to achieve your greater desire. This is why you have been asked to number the items.

Set your goals, make plans for the first steps towards achieving each goal, and, most important of all, begin now! Take the first step towards your goals today and make sure you do something towards your goals every day. Don't let yourself become distracted by other pursuits and pleasures. Be single-minded in fulfilling your deepest wants and needs and watch your life as it develops, progresses and flourishes in ways that please and satisfy.

Develop this new relationship with your inner self. Your intuition or inner wisdom is always available to you and will always give you an answer that is relevant to you and that you can trust. The answer may not arrive immediately and may even come on another day, but the answer *will* come and will always be appropriate and true for you. You will know the answer is right because you will have a feeling as thought a light has been switched on around the situation, a feeling of, "Oh yes! I understand", and a deep and warm feeling of certainty inside yourself.

Action Plan for Meeting Challenges

We all come up against challenges and difficulties in our lives from time to time. When this happens to you, rather than reacting hastily on the spur of the moment, you will find it better to use the tried and tested procedure that follows. This Action Plan will give you a framework for meeting the challenge successfully. It will allow you to stand back a little from the situation or difficulty, rather like an observer. By standing back you will then be able to respond in a more rational and effective way rather than reacting automatically with a possible escalation of feelings or rash, spur-of-the-moment actions. Then, with a calm mind, you can begin to seek the best solution to fit the situation.

There are five stages to the Action Plan.

1. 'STOP' and breathe, stay calm.
2. ACKNOWLEDGE and ACCEPT the challenge or difficulty.
3. ANALYSE the situation calmly.
4. ALTERNATIVES – look for and find.
5. ACTION to take – or non-action with acceptance.

And now, a brief explanation of each stage.

1. 'STOP'

When you find yourself faced with a difficulty or challenge, begin by saying to yourself, inside your head,

"STOP"

*and stop all thought and activity. Do not do anything immediately except concentrate on your breathing. Make your breathing deep, slow and steady. Now you are in control. Say to yourself, "Stay calm" or "I can cope with this", while you think what your response will be. Concentrate on your actions or **tactics**, not upon any uneasy feelings or thoughts you may have. Remember that fighting or suppressing thoughts and feelings only increases tension and fires the stress response. Instead, activate the relaxation response by keeping some of your attention on your breath as the situation develops. This will initiate a relaxed state of mind and allow access to cool thinking.*

2. ACKNOWLEDGE and ACCEPT the challenge or difficulty.

Calm, unemotional thought will also be more available to you when you can accept the situation as it is, without rejecting, judging or wanting to alter it in any way. Acceptance doesn't mean you either like the situation or are resigned to it, but that you accept it as it is, with acknowledgment that it is best to

Peaceful Sleep – when I say "peaceful sleep" I fall asleep easily and sleep right through the night

move on and begin afresh. With acceptance you recognise that you cannot change the past and that what has already been done or happened cannot now be altered. You let go of 'She/He/They/I shouldn't have........' and 'If only..........'

3. ANALYSE the situation calmly.

Once you have faced and accepted the situation, you will be in a position to analyse it calmly. Look at all aspects of the circumstances and, if it will make it clearer in your mind, write them down. Make a note of the background to what happened and the order of events. Then, ask yourself the following questions:

> *"What is the basic nature of the conflict?"*
>
> *"What is the fundamental purpose of the challenge?"*
>
> *"What is <u>my</u> fundamental purpose?"*
>
> *"What are the strengths of the challenge?"*
>
> *"What are <u>my</u> strengths?"*

4. ALTERNATIVES – look for and find.

Write down as many alternative actions as you can. Write at the top of a clean sheet of paper,

> *"What choices do I have?"*

and then jot down any responses that appear in your mind as to your possible courses of action. Trust your inner wisdom to produce the answers that are most appropriate for you. Keep asking this same question over and over until you have exhausted the supply of answers. Be flexible and open-minded. Write down anything that comes to your mind, no matter how preposterous; it may lead you on to a suggestion that will work. Always remember that to decide to discuss the matter with a colleague, friend or professional can also be an appropriate choice.

When you think you have completed your list, you could then ask this question which may produce yet more answers,

"What other *choices do I have?"*

5. ACTION to take – or non-action with acceptance
The final part of the Action Plan is to decide which of your choices to select for action. You may realise that there is no action you can take at the moment, but that will be a satisfactory answer in itself. Some situations need to be accepted just as they are. We cannot always find anything that can be done in a particular situation, other than to accept it as it is.

And so, decide upon your action, or non-action, by completing the statement,

"I have decided to ...."

If you are taking action of some kind, check out any resources you may need, such as materials or help from others. Cost them out and then set a date to start your plan. You can now take your action, confident in the knowledge that your inner wisdom has chosen wisely and well.

How to Cope with Challenges that can't be Solved

There will be some occasions when there doesn't seem to be an answer to a particular difficulty or challenge. There will always be some things in life we *can* change and some things we can't. Those that can't be changed for the moment are best accepted as they are, as we have already discussed. As you know, battling on against something when there is no hope of bringing about a change merely increases the stress response and causes you additional distress.

One valuable way to handle difficulties that appear to have no solution is to change your view of them and find another way of looking at them. See if you can turn the situation

Peaceful Sleep – when I say "peaceful sleep" I fall asleep easily and sleep right through the night

around and find positive aspects within it. For example, if your car has broken down and you can't use it for a week, instead of cursing and getting annoyed, take an active and positive pleasure in walking, sharing a lift with others or using public transport. Enjoy the different views you see and the different perspective on life you will gain. As a result, you may even end up taking a different daily route to work on a permanent basis. That is just a simple example but the basic method of handling the situation holds good whatever the circumstances.

Another way to deal with hard-to-solve challenges is to hand the whole problem over to a higher power, whether that be God, the Universe or just Time. It is best if you do this in a formal way to reinforce the decision in your subconscious mind.

Write your plight on paper and then shut it away in a drawer or box and say, as you shut the drawer or lid,

"I hand this over to you to deal with."

And then,

"I let this go............"

"All is well in my world."

Feel a sense of relief as the whole situation is taken out of your hands and passed over to another authority. Watch and wait and, in a while, you will come to see that the difficulty has been resolved, an answer has appeared or you will feel sufficiently energised from having given yourself a break to be able to deal with the challenge once again.

A further way to inject a note of positivity into a difficult situation is to use affirmations. This input of constructive and positive self-talk will soon help you to accommodate the situation. Choose simple and straightforward sentences that appeal to you and are relevant to your particular circumstances. Always repeat each affirmation with total conviction, as though it is really true for you at this very moment. Remember, you are not deceiving yourself, you are directing yourself towards how you wish to be. Select some appropriate affirmations from the following list, or make up your own. Repeat them wholeheartedly with *real feeling*.

"I can tolerate this while I seek a solution."

"I let this flow over me without it affecting me."

"I accept the situation, I go with it........"

"I move through life with ease and joy."

"I am the power and authority in my life."

"I am the power and authority to release the past and accept my good now."

"I love and approve of myself."

"I am happy to be me."

"I release thoughts of the past that has gone, and the future that has yet to come."

"I take one day at a time, and concentrate on what I am doing now."

"This is a great learning opportunity for me."

"I acknowledge my personal growth."

"I enjoy continuing to learn and to grow."

"It is easy for me to ...."

"I relax and let go..................."

"All is well in my world.'

And, finally, don't forget the therapeutic benefits of talking a difficulty over with friends, workmates or a professional, depending upon the level of feedback you need.

The Silver Cocoon

It's not normally a good idea to shut yourself off from people or occurrences but sometimes as a 'first aid' measure it may be useful to do so, especially if you cannot see any other immedi-

Peaceful Sleep – when I say "peaceful sleep" I fall asleep easily and sleep right through the night

ate way to handle a situation. The following technique will help you to feel in control and to give you a breathing space while you decide what to do. So, if you find you have difficulty in handling a particular happening or person, you might like to try 'protecting' yourself from their influence using the power of your imagination in this special way. This is another mental device, a mental 'trick' if you like, but that doesn't matter. If it works for you – USE it. Always be open and receptive to new ideas and give them a chance.

Imagine you are totally surrounded by sparkling, protective white light. Allow the light to flow all around you so that, if it could be seen, you would appear to be in a beautiful, transparent but shining, silvery capsule. Inside this shimmering aura of light you feel safe and secure from all outside influences. If you wish, you can imagine that the aura toughens and hardens, forming a thick, impenetrable barrier like a capsule, cocoon or shell all around you. You feel powerful and strong and completely protected inside the capsule or aura. You know that nothing can harm you, no words, no action. See yourself as a strong, indomitable person, totally in charge, totally at ease in whatever situation you find yourself. You can tell yourself, "I am powerful and invincible. I am in charge and I am the power in my life," and "I think calmly about what to do next."

See if you can maintain your protective aura or silver capsule in a situation that is not too difficult or threatening when you first practise. As with all skills, the more you practise, the more effective the technique will become. Be sure to follow the exercise with a question, such as, *'What choices do I have in handling this situation?'* to enable you actually to deal with the circumstances. You could use the Action Plan for Meeting Challenges earlier in this chapter to help you decide your action.

Practise the various techniques and ideas in this chapter and make a mental note to use them when appropriate. You will feel empowered with the knowledge that you now have the means to enrich your life in various nourishing ways. Taking charge of your life will overcome the negative effects of stress, and your sleep will gradually become more restful and tranquil. This developing balance and harmony in your life and caring attitude to yourself will be reflected in the quality of your sleep. Your inner being will sleep happily and peacefully and will have no need to gain your attention by disturbing your nights. Your reward will be a sense of wellbeing, vitality – and peaceful sleep at night.

Peaceful Sleep – when I say "peaceful sleep" I fall asleep easily and sleep right through the night

CHAPTER FIVE

Power-boosting Techniques and the Nature of Sleep

In this chapter you will discover some more power-boosting methods to ease the stresses in your daily life. These techniques will promote and maximise your own personal authority in your daily affairs. The first empowering process is time management. Time management and effective activity organisation will help you to reduce pressure in your life. There is a section with some relaxing physical exercises to use at bedtime to promote sleep, and another section with the indispensable Peaceful Sleep Action Plan for restless nights. You can also learn how to reduce dependency on sleeping pills, if that is of concern to you. The last section of the chapter contains some interesting and reassuring facts about the nature of sleep itself.

Time Management – Organising your Day

Many people find the pressure of time one of the prime causes of stress. There never seems to be enough time in the day for everything we either need or want to do, both in work and leisure. If this is your concern, you will benefit from planning your time more effectively and making sure that you also allow time for activities you enjoy.

1. Keep your life simple and stress-free by setting priorities (see below). This will help to reduce anxiety and to increase your efficiency.

2. Organise your time. You may even look at dropping certain things that are not as important, in order to do what you really want to do and the things you have to do. For instance, if time is limited, consider cutting the amount of TV you watch or the time spent on reading newspapers or magazines.

   Be flexible but stick to your underlying plan for your day based on the priorities you have decided upon. Avoid letting interruptions control your day and living by 'the seat of your pants'. Keep meetings to a minimum and set a time for their conclusion.

3. Always address the most demanding tasks first because you will be fresher and have more energy. Also, if you leave them till later, you may never get around to them and the pressure from not having completed your day's commitments will dominate your evening.

Peaceful Sleep – when I say "peaceful sleep" I fall asleep easily and sleep right through the night

4. Delegate where you can and remember that it is not an admission of inefficiency or weakness to ask for help when pushed for time.

5. Perfection is not achievable. Accept that you will make mistakes from time to time, it's only human to do so. Do what you can in the time you have allotted and then go on to your next priority.

6. Do your best and don't worry about events that are outside your control. This includes not feeling responsible for other people's behaviour.

7. Learn to say "no" when you either cannot or do not want to make time for something.

Priority Cards

It is essential to set priorities in your life in order to organise your day successfully and to reduce stress and anxiety. There is only so much you can achieve in a day and prioritising the issues in your life will enable you to use your time as effectively as possible. It is very simple to devise a card system to prioritise these issues, whether they are work, play or personal matters. Once you have determined which of your affairs are the most important you can concentrate on those activities and leave the rest for another designated occasion.

List the issues in your life that cause you concern and anxiety. Also list anything you need or want to do in the next few months.

Now write each item on a separate reminder card.

Arrange the cards in order of importance. Write on each card the date by which you want to deal with that particular subject.

At the beginning of each evening, rearrange your cards into their order of importance for the following day. You will be able to see at a glance which of your concerns to address tomorrow and which can be left for another day. At this time, you can, if need be, add cards containing new issues or remove cards that have been dealt with. It is useful to keep these finished cards in a separate pile as a reminder of your success.

By prioritising the issues in your life you will have less to worry about at bedtime. There will be fewer unresolved issues to think about and you will have a system to help you remember tasks you have to deal with in the future, thus taking away the worry about forgetting to remember a particular matter. You will feel in control and it will be a relief to know that you have a regular time each day to review your tasks, activities and other matters of concern to you. This is a wonderful stress-beating activity and is thoroughly recommended if you require structure to your day or if you are anxious at night about issues in your life. Now you can tell yourself, *"I have no need to think about that now, I <u>know</u> when I am going to deal with it."*

Saying 'No'

Everyone needs to be able to say "no" at times, whether to oneself or to others. Often we are 'people pleasers' and automatically agree to take on far more than we have time for. This can cause resentment and place pressure on you to complete yet another task in your busy day. Sometimes you may just need a space for yourself for a period of quietude and, again, this can easily be encroached upon by others unless you are firm. Saying "no" may feel rather strange and difficult at first, especially if you say it to people you care about. It is best if you say simply, in a straightforward manner,

"No, I'm sorry, I shall have to leave that for another time."

There's no need to offer explanations or apologies. People may be surprised when you first say "no" but you will gain their

Peaceful Sleep – when I say "peaceful sleep" I fall asleep easily and sleep right through the night

respect for having said what you really feel, and they will accept your refusal at face value, providing it is said firmly but kindly.

Physical Activities

Although vigorous exercise is not recommended near bedtime, there are some physical activities that can help to relax you and prepare you for sleep, such as gentle stretching, 'Rock-a-Bye', and the 'Shake-out'. Try them out and see if they help you. Take care if you have any physical problem at all – for example, rocking might not be suitable if you have a back problem. If in doubt, take the advice of your doctor or other health professional. Always make sure you are warm, comfortable and relaxed before starting any stretching exercises.

Rock-a-Bye

Try this exercise before you go to bed. Use an exercise mat or soft rug to protect your spine. Don't hurry with this exercise, the idea is to make the whole experience as relaxed as possible. Have the lights low, make sure you are warm and ready for bed.

Sit on the mat or rug and bring your knees up towards you with your hands clasped underneath them. Incline your head towards your knees, keep your back rounded and gently rock backwards and forwards. Rock for about six times and then lie on the floor in a relaxed position and enjoy some deep and slow breaths for a few minutes before going to bed.

It might be a good idea to do some gentle stretching exercises before you try the rocking to make sure your body is flexible and relaxed.

The 'Shake-out'

The 'Shake-out' breaks up patterns of repetitive body movements and helps to relax the nervous system. It is ideal for breaking up the downward spiral of anxiety and the 'stress response', and for those occasions when you seem caught with thoughts churning around in your mind. It is also useful if you have been doing one repetitive activity for a long time, such as typing or driving. With the 'Shake-out' you can give yourself a fresh, positive start.

1. *Take your shoes off and stand up (you could do it sitting if, for any reason, you are unable to stand). 'Ground' and 'centre' yourself for a moment or two by standing still and letting your feet sink into the ground as thought they are rooted in the earth. Take one or two slow deep breaths into your abdomen.*

2. *Very gently start to shake yourself, starting with your hands, then your arms and shoulders. Always be conscious of your feet being rooted into the ground.*

3. *Let your movements get bigger and bigger and gradually include your neck and head and then your whole body.*

4. *Allow your movements to be really uninhibited – like a rag doll or a puppet on strings. Let your arms fly in the air, your eyes roll! Open your mouth wide, pull faces and vocalise any sounds that may bubble up inside you. Just let go. Make really chaotic movements, movements as crazy and uncoordinated as you like. Have fun!*

5. *When you feel you've continued for long enough, shake out your feet, feel the vibrations right down to your toes and then STOP all activity and 'ground' and 'centre' yourself well before moving on to something new.*

   REMEMBER: *Keep your joints and muscles relaxed and loose all the way through and be conscious of your feet rooted to the ground.*

This exercise can be very demanding of your body, so take it easy the first few times you try it, especially if you have any

Peaceful Sleep – when I say "peaceful sleep" I fall asleep easily and sleep right through the night

physical problems. Do as much as you feel you can without overdoing things.

The 'Shake-out' is extremely valuable to use at night if you find you have been lying awake in bed and seem unable to relax. It will stop anxious, churning thoughts and tense physical sensations. You will notice the difference in how you feel immediately, as the exercise is truly excellent for dispelling negative thoughts and tense body patterns.

If you have done the 'Shake-out' at night, relax afterwards and perhaps do some gentle stretching. Go back to bed with a new, relaxed body and mind ready for sleep. Use the Peaceful Sleep Bedtime Routine (see Chapter 7) once you are in bed and you will soon drift down into a deep and peaceful sleep.

Dealing with Restless Nights

While we are training ourselves in any new skill we tend to make progress in an up-and-down fashion, rather than in a straight line. Until the Peaceful Sleep Bedtime Routine is firmly established, don't worry if you still have some restless nights. When you do, stay calm. Having an odd unsettled night does *not* mean that more will be bound to follow.

When you wake in the night, there is nothing to distract you. This leaves your mind free to pick up on negative thoughts and feelings. Knowing exactly what to do in these circumstances is greatly self-supporting and will enable you quickly to return to your slumbers.

To reduce the impact of a restless night, prepare yourself with some of the ideas that follow. The ideas range from dealing with specific difficulties that may arise to giving yourself general comforting support. Make a selection from these ideas to design your own personal Peaceful Sleep Action Plan; you will then always be ready and prepared for a restless night.

The Peaceful Sleep Action Plan

On the next few pages are ideas for coping with restless nights. Write on separate small cards or pieces of paper a selection of techniques that you would find helpful, and add any ideas of your own. This will make up your *Peaceful Sleep Action Plan*. I suggest writing the ideas on small cards as you can easily keep them close to you and read them unobtrusively during the day. Reading from a small separate card also helps to focus your mind on each idea. Keep your *Peaceful Sleep Action Plan* cards near you, so that if you do have a disturbed night you will know what to do about it. Read your cards or list during the day to prepare and reassure yourself, and also at night if you are awake and need support. Reading the cards over and over will give you confidence and reinforce the ideas for peaceful sleep in your subconscious mind. You will find there is always at least one idea appropriate for any particular occasion that will make the difference between remaining sleepless or relaxing back into a deep and peaceful sleep.

Ideas for your Peaceful Sleep Action Plan for Restless Nights

1. If you are awake, use the time in a positive way. Quiet relaxation is of great benefit and you may find that sleep creeps upon you unnoticed. Go through the Peaceful Sleep Body Scan in Chapter 2 again. While you are relaxing, your body will benefit from resting quietly and will begin the restoration process. (See the item, 'Compensating for Lost Sleep' later in this chapter.) Remember the 3 Rs and repeat to yourself,

   "As I relax and rest my body is being **restored***"*.

Peaceful Sleep – when I say "peaceful sleep" I fall asleep easily and sleep right through the night

2. You always sleep far more than you realise, probably three times more. Under no circumstances count the hours you *think* you have been asleep or awake, as this will undoubtedly lead to a flood of negative thoughts about coping with lack of sleep the next day. So, no more clock-watching! Cover or turn your clock so you can't see the time. Affirm,

"Time doesn't matter."
"I am totally adequate at all times."
"I know how to cope – I know, I'll concentrate on my breathing."

Focus always on your techniques and on what you are doing or feeling. Let go of any negative thoughts or feelings and NEVER, NEVER try to analyse the situation during the night.

3. If you become aware of thoughts going round and round in your head, say a firm "STOP!" to yourself and then CHANGE to a more appropriate thought or activity. Say to yourself,

*"**Tomorrow** is for thinking,*
***NOW** is for relaxing."*

For further details of this dynamic approach see Chapter 2.

4. REFUSE to listen to negative thoughts. Focus always on the positive aspects of your life, your blessings and strengths. The way we view our sleep and talk about our sleep affects the quality of our sleep. Say,

"I focus on the good things of today –
more good things will happen tomorrow."
"I seek and FIND happy positive thoughts."

5. If there is something specific worrying you, write it down, place the piece of paper in a drawer and when you shut the drawer affirm,

"I put my difficulties away at night. I will deal with them tomorrow."

Feel the sense of relief that comes when you hand the problem over to be taken care of on another day.

Continue this self-care by adding a powerful affirmation, such as,

*"It is safe to relax. It is **easy** for me to let go."*

6. Say 'STOP' and focus on your breathing. Give yourself a 'two-sighs' diaphragmatic breathing treat. SMILE as you breathe out, and keep that gentle smile on your face – relaxation starts with a smile. Each time your mind wanders, go back to your breathing. Refer to Chapter 2 for full details of the 'breathing treat'.

7. Another calming idea is to talk to yourself inside your head, as though comforting a small child. Reassure yourself that it's safe to relax, to let go, and to drift down into peaceful sleep.

8. Use your imagination to go on magical adventures. For instance, visit the Peaceful Sleep Garden or a tropical island, float away in a balloon, row across a calm pool, lie on a sandy beach or walk in a beautiful woodland. Visualise anything that is restful, enjoyable or amusing to you. See Chapter 2 for more details of visualisation.

9. Break a restless pattern of body or mind by getting up for a short while. Don't let self-pity in. Concentrate on finding something to soothe and comfort you. You can't be in control of everything. Just go with it, and look at yourself and the situation with compassion. Tell yourself,

"Peace, be still. This will pass. I know what to do."

10. If you decide to get up, do something relaxing, such as reading, listening to taped music or a story, or read your

Peaceful Sleep – when I say "peaceful sleep" I fall asleep easily and sleep right through the night

Peaceful Sleep Action Plan until you are ready to return to bed. If you feel very agitated or restless, break the pattern with the 'Shake-out' described in this chapter.

11. Try the 'Act as if..............' Technique. "If I was a person who slept peacefully all night – how would I be?" Act and pretend as though you are a person who always sleeps peacefully. Feel your body and mind relax, let go, and become peaceful. Chapter 4 gives you full details of this empowering technique.

12. Lastly, do not forget the gentle power of meditation as described in Chapter 4. Concentrate on your breathing as it flows in and out and let all other thoughts and feelings pass by without becoming involved with them. Breathe into any negative thoughts and feelings that arise. This is your reality at the moment, not the future or the past. Accept it. Let the thoughts and feelings float by, watch them dispassionately.

Keep your Peaceful Sleep Action Plan cards near you and take time when you have a break in your day to sit quietly and read through them. Do this often.

REMEMBER: *The more you practise the ideas, the techniques and the Peaceful Sleep Bedtime Routine, the more successful you will be and the sooner you will be sleeping peacefully right through **every** night.*

How to Reduce the use of Sleeping Pills

These days, we are more aware of the problems that can arise from taking drugs for sleep and many people are searching for a more acceptable option. Pills are useful for some occasional short-term problems, but not for longer-term insomnia as they don't tackle the underlying reason for the poor sleep and so can never provide a complete answer. Anyone can become dependent upon sleeping pills and it can happen far more quickly than you may realise. People can begin to rely on sleeping pills after only a few consecutive nights of taking them. It can happen very easily to absolutely anyone. We can all become used to relying on many different substances in our daily lives – coffee and tea, for example. Dependency, therefore, can creep up unnoticed, so that when someone wants to reduce their reliance upon them it can seem a very formidable challenge. If you decide you would like to reduce your sleeping pill intake, here are some suggestions as to how to go about it.

Discuss your desire to reduce your sleeping pills with your doctor. Ask for a prescription for a smaller quantity of pills, and ask for them to be made up in a reduced dosage size so that you can cut down more easily. For example, if you are now taking 10mg of a particular drug at night, ask for the pills in, say, a 2mg size. Each 10mg dose will now consist of five of the 2mg tablets which will make it easier for you to taper off your use gradually.

Make it easy on your body by cutting down your intake over a period of three or four months, and never take less than six to eight weeks to reduce.

Write down a proposed reduction plan phased over three or four months and show it to your GP or physician.

Reduce the amount of drug you are taking in small steps only. If you find it too demanding, you're cutting down too fast.

Be prepared for any withdrawal symptoms, such as a temporary increase in disturbed nights, with extra relaxation sessions so that you will at least be resting and relaxed in bed.

Drink plenty of water to help detoxify your body.

Take extra vitamins, especially vitamin C as found in fresh fruit and vegetables.

Cut down on other stimulants, such as coffee and colas, while you are reducing your pill intake.

Peaceful Sleep – when I say "peaceful sleep" I fall asleep easily and sleep right through the night

Increase your input of self-supporting and nurturing thera-pies, such as relaxing baths, massage and relaxation exercises.

Taking additional exercise during the afternoon will help to tire you and promote sleep at night.

Have the attitude of 'one day at a time'. Tell yourself that just for today you can manage with a lower dose/no pill. You can let tomorrow take care of itself.

Success breeds success, so praise yourself and tell yourself how well you are doing when you succeed in your day's aim. This will encourage you to continue your reduction pro-gramme. Ask yourself why you succeeded on a particular night and see if there is any reason for it that you can repeat on another night.

Keep a check list or diary of your progress and note any rea-sons for your failures as well as your successes.

Don't worry if you find you are 'stuck' on a lower dose and don't seem to be able to reduce this amount further. You have suc-ceeded so far and can always try again later when you have sta-bilised.

Contact a helpline if you feel you need additional support (see addresses at the end of the book).

Reducing sleeping pills is a big challenge but it is one you can win with determination, a properly prepared plan and the extra support you can give yourself with the relaxing and self-nourishing techniques in this book.

Sleep Training

The Sleep Training method is one final, if radical, way to improve sleep if it is very broken and disturbed. With this method, you train yourself to sleep solidly for the total number of hours that you currently sleep during an interrupted night. For example, if you average, say, about five hours of erratic sleep in all, you can train yourself to sleep those five hours in just one unbroken sleep session. Your mind and body will then become used to sleeping soundly and solidly in one block, rather than in short, restless bursts. You will then gradually, over a period of weeks, be able to lengthen the amount of time you are sleeping.

This is how Sleep Training works:

By referring to your Sleep Diary, add up the total hours of broken sleep you have over a week. Divide this total by seven. This will give you an average number of hours slept each night – say five hours.

If you need to get up at, say, 7.00am, subtract your five hours from 7.00am. This will give you a bedtime of 2.00am. This may seem to you to be a terribly late time to go to bed – but perservere.

If, after going to bed, you are still awake after 10 or 15 minutes, get up and do a quiet activity until you feel ready to go to sleep, then return to bed. Whatever happens happens. Even if you do not go to sleep at all, do not lie in past your morning waking time of 7.00am. In this way, you will gradually train your body to go to sleep when you go to bed.

When you have achieved your aim of getting five hours' sound sleep at night for a week or so, try increasing your sleep time by going to bed fifteen or twenty minutes earlier – at, say, 1.45am – for a week or so. Continue like this, making small increases to your total sleep time. To avoid setbacks, let each addition stabilise for five or six days before increasing your sleep time again.

Spread your Sleep Training over a period of at least six to eight weeks.

When your sleep eventually becomes disturbed again, it means that you've reached your optimum level. In other words, you've now arrived at the correct bedtime for you and will, in future, hopefully, be sleeping for a full night every night.

Peaceful Sleep – when I say "peaceful sleep" I fall asleep easily and sleep right through the night

This method requires great determination at the outset as you may find it very hard actually to stay awake until your 'bedtime'. However, it is essential that you do remain up and alert until your allotted time for bed. Another point is that, when you do eventually get to bed, you may find, having kept yourself awake for so long, that it is now hard for you to get to sleep! Nevertheless, with perseverance, the Sleep Training method does work. It has a proven track record of great success and is the chosen procedure in sleep clinics with people who, having tried all other methods, still have difficulty in sleeping.

Sleep Stages

The final section of this chapter is devoted to discussing what happens during your sleep. It is useful to learn about the different types of sleep you have each night and to discover along the way some reassuring facts.

Over the years, hundreds of studies of sleep have been made, examining brainwave activity during the day and the night. Sleep habits and sleep patterns have been carefully recorded and analysed.

Our brainwaves vary according to what we are doing. During the day, when we are involved in using our logical, thinking mind, our brainwaves make short, very active zigzag-like patterns on the measuring equipment. When we are asleep, our brainwave activity alternates between three basic types. The deeper the sleep, the slower the brainwaves, and the bigger and more spaced out are the zigzag patterns.

When we first become drowsy our muscles relax, our internal body processes begin to quieten down and our brainwaves become slower. This is called *light sleep*. Much of the night is spent in light sleep. *This is how our brain operates when we daydream, visualise or meditate.* This information will be useful to remember, as you will see shortly.

As we gradually drift further and further down into the deepest form of sleep, *deep sleep*, our brainwave patterns are at their most slow. Deep sleep is essential for our body's recovery and restoration from the wear and tear of the previous day's activities. Healing takes place during deep sleep with the release of a growth hormone which rejuvenates all the cells of our body. Most deep restorative sleep occurs early in the night.

From time to time, during light sleep and deep sleep, brain activity comes into frenzied life as we enter *dream sleep* or *REM sleep* (REM stands for Rapid Eye Movement). As we dream, our eyes move rapidly and this can be observed by anyone watching someone in dream sleep. If you see a dog or cat twitching and their eyelids flickering when they are asleep, they are in REM sleep and are dreaming.

We move through the entire cycle of sleep four or five times during the night. Most of our deep sleep comes in the first few hours of sleep and most of our dream sleep occurs in the latter part of the night when we are sleeping more lightly, which is why we are more likely to remember dreams that occur in the morning.

We normally spend about an hour in deep sleep *and* one to two hours in dream sleep *throughout the night. The rest of our sleep is* light sleep.

This is important to know, as you will see when you read about compensating for lost sleep.

Compensating for Lost Sleep

If you lose sleep, your body naturally compensates for the sleep loss by taking more, deep restorative sleep *the next night, although you are unaware that this is taking place. Even if you*

Peaceful Sleep – when I say "peaceful sleep" I fall asleep easily and sleep right through the night

sleep for only a few hours the next night, you will still be obtaining the necessary amount of deep sleep to make up your loss.

You will also have about 50% more dream sleep to compensate for that lost the previous night. The sleep you do lose is light sleep and it appears unnecessary to replace this.

It is very reassuring to know that you don't need to match hour for hour of lost deep and dream sleep on 'recovery' nights. Your body naturally compensates for lost sleep the next night, even though you are unaware of it. Trust your body to take care of its essential needs.

In scientific experiments, even when deprived of sleep for 8 – 11 days, most of the body's organs still function very well. The ill effects of loss of sleep are temporary, and your body is capable of full recovery. The brain itself needs rest but the rest of the body copes very well without sleep provided it has regular food *and regular rest.* You might feel as though you would like more sleep but, provided you have a few hours' of sleep and spend the rest of the time resting and relaxing in bed, there will be no long-term harm.

If you are awake at night, you can obtain the rest you need to cope with the loss of light sleep by using the Peaceful Sleep Body Scan, visualisation or meditation techniques to ensure that you obtain optimum rest for your body even if you are not asleep. Brainwaves during these types of relaxation are similar to those during light sleep and are a good substitute for that element of your sleep.

You're getting more sleep than you Realise

If you *think* you haven't had enough sleep, you will *feel* as though you haven't had enough sleep. This is because your beliefs and what you tell yourself make up your reality. However, we all tend to be inaccurate in judging how much sleep we've had because it is very easy to misjudge time at night. You can be assured that you *are* sleeping far more than you realise, probably about three times more!

Scientific studies proved that, although volunteers in a study group thought they had taken a very long time to fall asleep initially and had been awake for hours during the night, this was not, in fact, true. The equipment used to measure the volunteers' sleep showed they had fallen asleep within fifteen minutes and had then been deeply asleep for most of the night, although they said they thought it had taken them an hour or more to go to sleep and that they had been awake for much of the night. They had actually had about *three times* more sleep than they had perceived.

Misconception about the length of time we have slept can be very disturbing. It's certainly difficult to convince someone that they have been asleep for the majority of the night when they think they've been wide awake for much of the time. If this is true of you and if you tend to tell yourself that you haven't slept a wink all night, you can now question this belief, because, as you have seen, you will, in fact, have been sleeping for far longer than you originally thought. Say to yourself, and believe it, *"I've slept for far longer than I'm aware."* As a result, you may then find that you actually *feel* better.

How Much Sleep Do You Need?

The length of time you need to sleep will vary according to your age and your own individual personal requirements, which change throughout your life. As a baby, you need about fifteen hours out of every twenty-four. As a teenager you no doubt feel you could often sleep happily until midday, given the opportunity. As an adult you will have your own individual sleep needs which range somewhere between six to ten hours of sleep a night. However, there are still wide variations outside this. For instance, Winston Churchill needed only four hours sleep and, at the other end of the scale, Albert Einstein

Peaceful Sleep – when I say "peaceful sleep" I fall asleep easily and sleep right through the night

needed far more than average to perform well during the day. As we become older adults we seem to need less sleep, our sleep is lighter and we are more easily woken. Once we realise that this broken sleep is the normal pattern, we can accept it and not worry about it.

To know for how long you need to sleep, judge your sleep requirement against the Peaceful Sleep Ideal in the Introduction to this book. If you feel refreshed, full of vitality in the morning and have enough energy for what you want to do throughout the day then you are having enough sleep. If you find yourself falling asleep during the day within five minutes or so of quietly sitting or lying down, you probably did not have enough sleep the previous night.

Dreams

Our dreams seem to achieve the same for our minds as deep sleep does for our bodies. Dreams send 'messages from the unconscious' to make us aware of unresolved problems, or suggest answers to those problems. Dreams also appear to have the function of smoothing our emotional life. The old adage of 'sleeping on it' in relation to a problem has some truth in it. Our subconscious mind seems to go to work at night, using our dreams to help us feel in a different mood in the morning and more able to meet any challenges in our life. Dreams can even be creative, providing material for music, art and writing. Professor Francis Crick of San Diego believes dreams are a way for the brain to have a 'spring clean' of old, unwanted information. He thinks the mind sorts through material to either store it or lose it, rather like a computer.

Dreams can occur during any of the different types of sleep we have. Nature is very efficient and, as we rarely remember our dreams, presumably Nature doesn't intend us to remember them unless there is a message about which we need to be aware. Dreams may be your mind's way of nudging you into taking action about some unresolved matter. Unpleasant, recurring dreams may be your mind's way of drawing your attention to something in your life that needs to be dealt with. This may be something you are unhappy about at a deep level, a current relationship that is causing problems or a traumatic event from the past. You may be able to unravel the meaning of your dreams by keeping a dream diary. The meaning of dreams can become clear as you write them down.

Keeping a Dream Diary

Keep a notebook and pencil at your bedside and, as soon as you awake and your dream is fresh in your mind, jot down its outline. Do this as fast as you can as the dream will soon evaporate. Keep your diary for two weeks and at the end of that time sift through your record and see if there are any recurring themes. Not all dreams are important. Some reflect the events of the last few days and you will quickly pick those out, but others may be of more significance. Our dreams tend to contain symbols rather than a direct message. So, for example, if you dreamed you were driving a car which was going too fast, was it something you saw on TV or do you think it signifies that you feel your life is out of control? Check your dreams against what is going on in your life and see if you can find an interpretation of your dreams that resonates with you. You don't need a book of dream interpretations; no-one will know better than you what your dreams signify, as we all have individual, personal symbols for our inner self's messages. All you require to be your own dream interpreter is a dash of imagination together with the ability to ask yourself honest questions and to be open to any answers that may arrive.

Peaceful Sleep – when I say "peaceful sleep" I fall asleep easily and sleep right through the night

Summary

1. Use time management skills to reduce stress and increase efficiency.

2. Set priorities and make Priority Cards.

3. Learn how to say 'no' to extra demands.

4. Be aware that relying on sleeping pills can cause dependency. Reduce your intake with the cooperation of your GP and a structured programme set over three or four months.

5. Try physical activities such as gentle stretching, rocking or the 'Shake-out' to prepare you for sleep.

6. Compile your own Peaceful Sleep Action Plan against the possibility of a disturbed night.

7. If you have a poor night, a few hours' sleep with the remainder of the time spent in rest and relaxation in bed will take care of your body's basic sleep needs. Your body will come to no harm and is capable of full recovery from loss of sleep.

8. We all tend to misjudge how much sleep we get at night. You are getting far more sleep than you think you are, probably about three times more.

9. Even though you are unaware of it, your body automatically compensates for lost sleep by taking extra the next night. It is not necessary for the lost sleep to be matched hour for hour.

10. Keep a dream diary to discover more about your own inner world and to understand what is going on in your life.

CHAPTER SIX

The Peaceful Sleep Approach to the Day and the Night

This last chapter takes the form of an accessible reference of ideas for transforming and promoting sleep.
The chapter takes you, step by step, through your day
and night with specific ideas for each time of the day, from
awakening in the morning to 'winding down' near bedtime.
The rundown of information will remind you how to look
after your energy levels and stay relaxed during the day so that
there is no build-up of stress and adrenaline levels towards
bedtime. The chapter number is given as a reference next to
those techniques which have been described in full elsewhere
in this book so that you can refresh your memory about any

particular item. The aim is for you to construct a balanced and harmonious day that will lead naturally to inviting peaceful sleep at night, and to build a cycle of confidence in yourself and your sleep, where success builds upon success.

Come back to this section time and time again, both as a reminder and also for fresh ideas while you develop your sleep-promoting campaign.

First thing in the Morning

1. Note your first thoughts and feelings, whatever they are. These first thoughts of the day often give an illuminating glimpse into your state of mind. If your thoughts and feelings are positive, if you feel excited about the day ahead, that's wonderful. If thoughts and feelings are more negative, that's fine too, just note them and then let them go. Use some inspiring affirmations to greet the day positively.

(Chapter 2)

2. Let some of your first thoughts be in praise of yourself for the way the night was handled by you. Use the transforming power of affirmations to boost your confidence and self-esteem. Choose from the affirmations below or make up appropriate ones of your own.

"I let this night go, I enjoy the day and accept what it will bring."

"I have many skills and am learning more daily."

"I love and approve of myself."

"Today is a fresh start, I greet it with joy."

"All is well in my world."

"Today is MY day." (Chapter 2)

3 If you are keeping a dream diary, your first action as soon as you have greeted the day is to jot down any fragments from your dreams that you can remember. You need to be quick about this, as dreams are very elusive and will soon

disappear from your memory. A dream diary will help you to discover more about your own inner world and give you an understanding about what is going on in your life.

(Chapter 5)

4. A consistent and regular routine is all-important in ensuring good, healthy sleep, so respect your inborn sleep pattern by getting up at the same time each day, including weekends and on holidays. You may be tempted to have a lie-in, but if you take more sleep than you need or disrupt the routine of your assigned waking hour, it may be harder to get to sleep the following night.

5. It is best if your waking up routine is gentle and easy, but for those of you who don't find it easy to wake up in the morning, try putting an alarm clock at the other side of the room so that you have to get up to turn it off. If it is dark, switch the light on immediately you wake up as this will help you to feel wide-awake.

6 If you are keeping a sleep diary, fill it in for the previous night as soon as you are alert. It's easy to forget to complete the diary if you leave it for later in the day.   (Chapter 3)

7. Before you get up each day, ask yourself, *"What am I going to do to-day to enjoy myself?"* Make sure you find time during the day to participate in your chosen activity.

8. Finally, before you arise, give yourself some 'breathing treats' and practise some deep diaphragmatic breathing. These will do wonders for your wellbeing and set a relaxed tone for the day. Use the 'two-sighs' method. This method is so important, I give it in full here:

Take a deep breath and then let it out fully with your mouth open wide, let the breath out with a sigh. Imagine the breath

Peaceful Sleep – when I say "peaceful sleep" I fall asleep easily and sleep right through the night

going from the top of your head down to your abdomen. Let it all out right down to the very last bit of air. Feel your abdomen contract as the old stale air is pushed out. Close your mouth and let the in-breath come of its own accord. Notice how your diaphragm pops up with the intake of breath.

Breathe like this once more and, this time, imagine that your breath travels from the top of your head right down to your feet and into the earth, with a sigh.

Then lie still and just enjoy a few moments of deep and natural breathing through your nose. This 'two-sighs' deep diaphragmatic breathing 'kick starts' your breathing mechanism into breathing from the abdomen. It ensures that you are breathing correctly from the abdomen and not from the chest. Deep diaphragmatic breathing can release all tension and stress and will set you up with the right frame of mind for the day. Remember to use this quick and easy breathing programme often during the day to avoid a build-up of stress. (Chapter 2)

The Peaceful Sleep approach to the Day

1. During the day use time management skills to make sure you aren't overworking, to reduce stress and to increase efficiency. Learn how to say a gentle but firm 'no' to extra work and commitments if they are too demanding on your time. Create space in your day that is just for you, and use it to recharge your batteries and to reconnect with nature. Make sure you also take time out of your busy day for enjoyment and fun.

2. Keep your life simple and stress-free by setting priorities. Reduce anxiety and increase your efficiency by organising your tasks and activities into order of importance to be dealt with. Make or read your Priority Cards. If you have any specific anxieties, deal with them either during the day or in the early part of the evening so they will be less likely to impinge on your sleep.

Write down anything that you cannot deal with immediately and set the cards aside until you are ready to deal with them. Include the first step you will take, and the date when you will take it. (Chapter 5)

3. Take plenty of regular daytime exercise. A good time to exercise (which can be just a brisk walk) is in the late afternoon. It's best not to exercise vigorously in the evening as this will boost adrenaline levels which will inhibit sleep.

4. Take your meals at regular times and eat wholesome, well-balanced food with plenty of fresh fruit and vegetables. It's not advisable to have a heavy meal late in the evening as the digestion process may keep you awake.

5. Make sure you take relaxation breaks during the day, at lunch time at the minimum. It's important to get right away from your work and spend some time, at least 15 – 20 minutes, quietly in relaxation or meditation. If there is no other opportunity during the day for relaxation, practise the Peaceful Sleep Bedtime Routine at lunch time. Remember that relaxation and letting go are central to reducing stress in your body and mind. (Chapters 2 and 4)

6. Remember to give yourself some deep diaphragmatic breathing 'treats' often during the day. Use the 'two-sighs' method described in No. 8 of the previous section.
(Chapters 6 and 2)

7. Be careful not to take naps during the day. If you feel sleepy after lunch take a quick walk outside or practise deep breathing near an open window.

8. Your thoughts are powerful. Challenge negative thoughts as they arise. Focus on the positive aspect of life, always.

Peaceful Sleep – when I say "peaceful sleep" I fall asleep easily and sleep right through the night

Use the 'STOP and CHANGE' technique when you become aware of negative thoughts in your mind. Step back and think rationally, ask yourself,

"Is this really true?"
"What is the worst that can happen?"
"Am I helping myself thinking this?"   (Chapter 2)

9. Continue your input of positive affirmations throughout the day, especially the Peaceful Sleep Affirmation.

(Chapter 2)

Winding Down in the Evening

Use the following analysis session as the marker between daytime activities and winding-down activities for the evening. This is the time to let go of the day, having dealt with any uncomfortable issues.

1. In the evening, well ahead of the last hour before bedtime, which should always be kept sacred for sleep preparation only, reserve thirty minutes or so to check your Priority Cards and to work on letting go of any problems or anxieties you currently may have. With any challenges that are of concern to you, write down the next constructive step you will take, and when you will take it. It's important not to leave loose ends, as these are the issues that will reappear in worry form when you want to sleep. You needn't actually sort out any of the matters, merely refer them to a better time to deal with them.   (Chapter 5)

2 If there are any items that continue to be of concern to you, hand them over to another power to deal with: your subconscious mind, your own inner wisdom, Time, God, Universal Energy, or whatever particular source resonates with you. Write the concern on a piece of paper and shut it away in a drawer in another room away from the bedroom. Notice the relief as you hand over the issues, for the moment, to this

other authority. Doing this will give you respite and allow the matter to be viewed in a different light at a future date.

3. Often, in order to move on, we need to have an attitude of forgiveness towards someone – sometimes ourselves. Forgiveness sets us free, it allows us to leave the past behind and to make progress. To forgive, all you need is the *desire* and *intention* to forgive. You could add a liberating affirmation, such as, *"I forgive and let go"* or *"I release anything that is not love from my life."*

4. During your winding-down period avoid anything stimulating, including foods and drinks, activities, exercise, work and arguments. If you play music, make it gentle and soothing, avoiding loud, discordant sounds.

5. It's best not to have a late or heavy meal approaching bedtime, so avoid highly-spiced, sugary and fatty foods. On the other hand, make sure you aren't hungry. Some people find a light, easily digestible snack helpful before going to bed. Find out what suits you best. Try lettuce soup or lettuce sandwiches; lettuce is said to have a soporific effect.

6. Smoking, like alcohol, is a stimulant and is best avoided for at least five hours before your go to bed. You are more likely to wake up in the very early hours of the morning if you have indulged in either smoking or alcohol. Also, it's best to avoid all caffeine-containing drinks and foods; these include colas, coffee, tea and chocolate.

7. Some people find certain drinks have a sedative effect. You could try milk, as it contains a natural sedative, tryptophan, which aids restfulness. Or try a malted food drink or herbal tea, such as valerian or chamomile, at bedtime. However, if you find you have to get up in the night, con-

Peaceful Sleep – when I say "peaceful sleep" I fall asleep easily and sleep right through the night

sider limiting your liquid intake during the evening with nothing to drink after about 6.00 p.m.

8. Make sure your bed and bedding are comfortable and warm but not hot, and that your bedroom is warm enough, yet well aired.

9. Strengthen your body rhythms by keeping regular hours. With this in mind, get up and go to bed at the same time each day. Your body can 'learn' what time you want it to go to sleep and wake up. (Think of the times you wake just before the alarm clock goes off!)

10. Use bed and bedroom for sleep only. Don't watch TV, listen to the radio, read, work, smoke or eat in bed. Don't discuss work or domestic or relationship problems in bed. Your subconscious mind will gradually accept the idea that when you go to bed it is time for you to go to sleep.

11. Be aware that relying on sleeping pills can cause dependency. Reduce your intake with the cooperation of your GP or physician and a structured programme set over three or four months.   (Chapter 5)

12. A warm and soothing bath with some aromatic essential oils, such as lavender, sandalwood or rose, will help you to relax at bedtime.

13. Try some gentle stretching exercises. The relaxation process is encouraged with gentle stretching of your body and limbs. Hold each stretch for thirty seconds or so – but hold the stretch, not your breath! Remember to keep breathing gently whilst holding the stretch.

14. Ensure your mind is in a positive and loving groove before you go to bed. Banish worry thoughts and thoughts which reduce your self-esteem and confidence. Instead, spend some time praising yourself and appreciating the positive happenings of the day. Make a list of all the good things

from your day – either a written or mental list. List everything and anything you can think of, not just big things, but tiny events too, such as taking a moment to appreciate the smell or colour of a flower, or a beautiful sunset. Praise yourself for being open to new coping skills and for giving yourself this loving attention.

15. Spend the last hour or so of the evening actually preparing for sleep. Keep activities low-key and undemanding so that you are in a relaxed and quiet mood when it is time for bed but don't become so relaxed that you fall asleep on the sofa.

16. Establish a ritual at bedtime for this last hour, for example:

> *Bath*
> *Stretch exercises*
> *Acknowledge the 'good' from the day*
> *Praise and appreciate yourself*
> *Affirmations*
> *Drink*
> *Clean teeth*
> *Bed*
> *Massage forehead and abdomen* (see below)

and finally

the Peaceful Sleep Bedtime Routine.

In Bed

1. Try massaging the 'sleep' points on your body. The two major points that relate to sleep are in the centre of your forehead and the lower part of your abdomen. If you can, massage the points at the same time, in a gentle and slow

Peaceful Sleep – when I say "peaceful sleep" I fall asleep easily and sleep right through the night

circular motion, your hand on your abdomen moving in a clockwise direction, (moving down the left side and up the right side of your abdomen) and your other hand on your forehead moving in the opposite direction. By concentrating on the two points at the same time, you will ensure that your mind is fully anchored in the here and now and so cannot think other thoughts.

2. When in bed, lie still. Try not to fidget or toss and turn from side to side, as that will remind your brain that you are awake.

3. Begin the Peaceful Sleep Bedtime Routine. Think yourself, step by step, through the Routine inside your head. It doesn't matter if you miss parts out or don't get the order quite right, the more you practise during the day, the easier you will find it when you go through the Routine at night. If you come to the end of the Routine and are still awake, just commence at the beginning again, either at the very start or with the Body Scan.   (Chapter 7)

4. If you don't fall asleep within 10 minutes or so of completing the Peaceful Sleep Bedtime Routine get up and do something else in another room. Don't go back to bed until you are ready to fall asleep. The same applies if you wake in the middle of the night for any length of time. Don't associate your bedroom with lying awake. Get up, make a warm drink, write letters, read, or involve yourself in some other quiet activity until you are ready to go to sleep again.

5. Finally, while you are still learning your new routines, you may still have the occasional restless night. If so, stay serene and remember you have all the skills you need at your fingertips. All you need do is refer to your Peaceful Sleep Action Plan, as described in the last chapter, and you will be sure to find something there to comfort and reassure you, to enable you to go back to sleep with an untrou-

bled mind. Keep your Peaceful Sleep Action Plan near you during the day and the night, it will be your friend and support at times of need. It is reassuring just to know that you have such a friend, even if you never make use of it.

In the next chapter, you can read a full description of the Peaceful Sleep Bedtime Routine, the wonderfully powerful method that is at the heart of your campaign for peaceful sleep.

Peaceful Sleep – when I say "peaceful sleep" I fall asleep easily and sleep right through the night

CHAPTER SEVEN

How to use the Peaceful Sleep Bedtime Routine

Use the Peaceful Sleep Bedtime Routine each night when you wish to go to sleep. You will quickly learn this simple Routine which will allow sleep to come over you easily and naturally. You will go to sleep knowing you will awake wonderfully refreshed, relaxed and full of energy ready to enjoy the day.

The magical visualisation in the Peaceful Sleep Bedtime Routine will allow you to enter a secret world of your very own creation. In this inner world you will have the opportunity to make undreamed-of changes in your life. You will actually go to sleep not in your own bed but, in your imagination, in the Peaceful Sleep Bed, the most safe and comfortable bed in the whole world, where you are sure to sleep peacefully all through the night.

Visualisation is a powerful tool and a real therapy in that it can help you make beneficial changes in your body. It is also enjoyable and fun! Everyone can visualise. If you need to remind yourself of the benefits of visualisation and relaxation, these are covered in Chapter 2. Remember that, when visualising, most people have either fleeting pictures in their mind or flashes of sensations in their body, rather than continuous pictures in their mind as though they were watching a film. Whichever way you visualise is just fine and is right for you. You can use your imagination to visualise either real events and objects or imaginary places and happenings.

The Peaceful Sleep Bedtime Routine is so relaxing that you may never actually complete it, you may fall asleep almost immediately. However, if you do come to the end of the Routine and are not yet asleep, just start again at the beginning and sleep will soon creep upon you. You can repeat the Peaceful Sleep Bedtime Routine as many times as necessary.

Outline of the Peaceful Sleep Bedtime Routine

Going through the Peaceful Sleep Bedtime Routine is rather like telling yourself a story. This story is very simple. When you want to go to sleep you will take two deeply relaxing breaths, repeat the Peaceful Sleep Affirmation and then begin the Peaceful Sleep Bedtime Story by imagining you are entering a beautiful Secret Garden that is yours alone. Within the garden you find a special house, the House of Dreams, which is, again, just for you. In the house is the Peaceful Sleep Bed. It is in this bed, the most wonderfully comfortable bed in the whole world, that you begin the Peaceful Sleep Body Scan and drift off to sleep.

Peaceful Sleep – when I say "peaceful sleep" I fall asleep easily and sleep right through the night

When you tell yourself the Peaceful Sleep Bedtime Story you can, of course, enlarge upon the basic outline above, filling in the story with as much detail as you like. The visualisation that follows is my very own, the one that I tell myself. **Please don't attempt to learn the visualisation by heart.** It doesn't matter in the least if your version isn't exactly the same as mine. Read through my visualisation a few times and you will soon get the general idea and be able to take yourself through your own story quite confidently. Use my ideas if you wish and make your story as simple or as complicated and detailed as you like. Create the Secret Garden and all that is within it as vividly and as clearly as you can.

NOTE: **Daytime practice of the Peaceful Sleep Bedtime Routine**

The Peaceful Sleep Bedtime Routine can also be practised during the day to help you to get to know your inner world. Daytime practice will allow you to explore fully your Secret Garden and the House of Dreams. If you so wish, during the day you could use a fuller Body Scan routine to help relax you before beginning the visualisation. **Please bear in mind that, as you may be tired, any relaxation or visualisation session held during the day may tempt you into falling asleep.** *Try not to let this happen if you are worried that it may reduce the amount of time you sleep at night.*

When you practise during the DAY, only take yourself to the point of going into the Peaceful Sleep Bedroom and sitting on the Peaceful Sleep Bed. Then lie or sit quietly for a few moments more and return to full alertness gradually, knowing that you can return to the Peaceful Sleep Bed at bedtime when you are ready for sleep. During daytime practice, be aware that you may feel very eager to remain in the Peaceful Sleep Bed just because it is so wonderfully comfortable and relaxing. You may also discover that, perhaps for the first time, you are actually looking forward with anticipation to bedtime because you will be able to sleep in this wonderful bed. This shift in attitude is obviously of immense benefit to you, and can in itself transform your sleep pattern.

The Peaceful Sleep Bedtime Routine

And now for my version of the Peaceful Sleep Bedtime Routine.

1. *Make yourself as comfortable as you can be, close your eyes and let your breathing become slower and deeper.*

2. *Let the next breath out with a slight sigh and imagine that it travels from the top of your head down to your abdomen.*

    Let the next breath out with a slight sigh and this time imagine that it travels from the top of your head right down to your feet.

3. *And now repeat the affirmation you've been practising, say it with real feeling,*

    "Peaceful sleep. When I say "peaceful sleep" I fall asleep easily and sleep right through the night."

    Repeat the affirmation once more and feel your body begin to let go. Feel waves of relaxation move through your body spreading softness and soothing warmth. Say "Relax" to your feet and legs, "Relax" to your back, and "Relax" to your head and face. Feel each area let go.

4. *You feel wonderfully relaxed and calm, and now that still-ness and peace are beginning to flow freely around your body, you are ready to use your imagination. **Take it slowly and gently, enjoy each part of the visulaisation fully. Spend time imagining everything in as much detail as you possibly can.***

Peaceful Sleep – when I say "peaceful sleep" I fall asleep easily and sleep right through the night

*See yourself standing in front of an old stone archway.
Through the archway you can see a beautiful garden – this is
your very own Secret Garden.*

*As you pass through the arch, imagine you are walking
through a shimmering, sparkling Curtain of Light. This dancing radiant shower or waterfall of white light washes away
every last trace of your day's cares and concerns, leaving you
cleansed, free and uplifted as you enter the Secret Garden.
Imagine the light dancing all around you like an aura as you
walk into the Garden. It is yours to keep with you whilst you
are here.*

*Now you are standing on a green, newly-mown lawn. You
pause for a moment and look around the Secret Garden. Take
your time to create the garden of your dreams in your imagination. Sense everything about it, the flowers, trees, birds, but-
terflies, water.*

*In the Secret Garden there are many special areas, each with
its own qualities to refresh, uplift and heal you. Look around
now and see the different areas: The Rainbow Flowerbeds to
fill you with healing and balancing energy. The Pool of Stars
with its magical reflection to give you confidence and self-
assurance in all you do. The wonderful Healing Fountain with
its magical droplets to fill you with vibrant, glowing health
and to ease away aches and pains. And the Tree of Wisdom
which can, when you touch it, pass to you its own strength,
power and knowledge. You can go to the Tree of Wisdom at
any time for answers to any questions you may have.*

*For now, just notice these special areas. On another occa-
sion, you can pay a visit to any of these areas to take advantage of their individual healing qualities.*

*Walk on through the Secret Garden down a grassy path
until you see ahead of you your House of Dreams. Construct
your house exactly as you would like it to be, whether your
House of Dreams is a cottage or a palace.*

Put your hand in your pocket and find in there the key to

the door – it has your name engraved upon it, it is the only key to the House of Dreams and it is YOURS. No-one but you is able to enter here, except by your specific invitation.

Open the front door and step inside. You immediately feel totally at peace and happy here.

The inside of the House of Dreams is exactly as you would desire it to be and you feel totally comfortable and at home. All the furniture, curtains, wall coverings and carpets are precisely as you would wish them to be.

In the House of Dreams there are various special rooms. There is the Future-Now Room where you can sit in a Golden Chair and watch the Silver Screen upon which you can see and practise future events and important meetings so that your performance will be smooth and confident. There is the Therapy Room where your healing powers will be phenomenal and you can have any treatment you desire. Come here at any time you have any ailment, from a sore throat to something more serious. Then there is the Fun Room where you can come to enjoy yourself and perfect any hobby, sport or craft.

On other occasions, you can visit all of these rooms and as many others as you wish to construct for yourself. For now just notice these remarkable rooms. There will be other opportunities for you to pay a special visit to any of them to take advantage of their individual healing qualities.

*Now you are going to go to a very special room – the Peaceful Sleep Bedroom – the bedroom of your dreams. You stand before the door which is surrounded and protected with its own shining, shimmering aura of silvery light. You open the door and go inside, taking some of the light with you. Here you feel **totally** safe, comfortable and peaceful, it's a place where you're always able to relax instantly. Look around the*

Peaceful Sleep – when I say "peaceful sleep" I fall asleep easily and sleep right through the night

room – it's a lovely place, so restful and quiet. Decorate it just as you would like it to be, with the furniture, curtains, carpets and everything else in it to your own taste. Take your time. Make everything in it as clear in your mind as you can.

In the room there is a big, comfortable bed – it's the most comfortable bed imaginable and it's just for you. It's the Peaceful Sleep Bed. Go and touch it, it's so soft and comfortable. Now sit down on the bed and feel its wonderfully soft support. You just KNOW you will be able to relax completely in this bed and sleep peacefully right through the night. You know you can have the sweetest dreams in this bed. You touch the pillow, it feels like fluffy white swan's-down under your hand. See the bed in your mind as clearly as you can.

And now climb on to the big comfortable Peaceful Sleep Bed and lie down. Feel your body sink down, the bed is as soft as the softest fleece. Let your whole body sink down, right down, into your wonderfully comfortable Peaceful Sleep Bed. You feel beautifully relaxed and peaceful here, you feel you can enjoy deep and peaceful sleep all night long.

Now, in the Peaceful Sleep Bed, begin the Peaceful Sleep Body Scan. Say, 'Peaceful Sleep' to each part of your body in turn. For example, place your mind on your left foot and say 'Peaceful Sleep'. Continue in this way all around your body, left and right feet in turn, calves, thighs, hips, lower back, abdomen, upper back, shoulders, neck, and all around your face. As you talk to each part of your body, let it feel heavy, relaxed and warm as it sinks down into your Peaceful Sleep Bed. Feel yourself sink further and further into the bed as you 'visit' each part of your body.

Feel your whole body filled with relaxation, you are totally serene and peaceful. You are wholly at ease. As you lie in the Peaceful Sleep Bed you feel so very serene and tranquil that it's easy to drift down into a deep and peaceful sleep until it's your time to awake. Just let go and allow yourself to drift down to sleep.

With daily use of the Peaceful Sleep Bedtime Routine, along with the transforming stress-reducing ideas in the rest of the book, you will soon be having the quality and amount of sleep you desire. Never forget that the peaceful, tranquil feelings generated by relaxation and visualisation are always there within you, waiting to be released. With the Peaceful Sleep Bedtime Routine you have the means of releasing those magical powers at bedtime when you need them most.

Remember that the Peaceful Sleep Bedtime Routine is available on audiotape, details of which are at the end of the book.

Peaceful Sleep – when I say "peaceful sleep" I fall asleep easily and sleep right through the night

Conclusion

With the ideas and techniques in this book you are offered the means of overcoming your insomnia and gaining peaceful sleep at night. The book approaches the challenge of sleeplessness on two fronts. Firstly, the unique relaxation and visualisation programme within the Peaceful Sleep Bedtime Routine has the capability of easing you into a deep and peaceful sleep at bedtime. Secondly, the ideas and techniques within the book will give you the means to tackle any underlying causes of your disturbed sleep pattern and allow you to make positive changes in your life.

As you now know, the way you live your day affects the quality of your sleep. The aim of this book is that, eventually, your days will be such that your path through life becomes one that is joyful and loving, where you treat yourself kindly and with respect, flow through your days with ease and grace, and live with your fellows in harmony and peaceful accord. When we use our time wisely and learn to view events more dispassionately we lead a balanced life in which sleep comes sweetly and naturally. By consistently using the practical and dynamic methods described, you will find that these positive changes arrive easily, bringing enrichment and equilibrium to your life. As you grow and flourish and become more in tune with yourself, your health and sleep will improve correspondingly.

When you consider making any changes in your life, go easy with yourself. Some of the recommendations are bound to work better for you or have a more immediate effect than others. If a technique seems rather challenging at first, try something easier to begin with, and keep referring back to the book for further information, ideas and encouragement.

Always remember that we move and grow towards that upon which we place our attention. So stay focused on the positive idea of sleeping peacefully in the Peaceful Sleep Bed, staying calm during the day and night and being gentle with yourself. Keep your mind on how you would like your sleep to be and on ways of helping yourself towards that goal, and you will achieve success. What you choose to think about really does decide your reality. Use the Peaceful Sleep Bedtime Routine daily and you will soon enjoy a full night's peaceful, restorative sleep and awaken refreshed and ready with enthusiasm and vigour to greet each day as a new opportunity.

I wish you peaceful days and peaceful sleep at night – every night.

Peaceful Sleep – when I say "peaceful sleep" I fall asleep easily and sleep right through the night

Further Reading

Borysenko, Joan, *Minding the Body, Mending the Mind*, Bantam, 1988

Dawes, N and Harrold F., *Massage Cures*, Thorsons, 1990.

Clayton, Dr Paul, *Stop Counting Sheep – Self-help for Insomnia Sufferers*, Headline, 1994.

Courtenay, Anthea, *Natural Sleep – How to Beat Insomnia without Drugs*, Thorsons, 1990.

Empson, Dr Jacob, *Sleep and Dreaming*, Harvester Wheatsheaf, 1993.

Holford, Patrick, *Vitamin Vitality*, Collins, 1985

Lake, T., *Living with Grief*, Sheldon Press, 1984. (self-help for dealing with bereavement and loss.)

Lambley, Dr P. *Insomnia and Other Sleeping Problems: A Self-help Guide to Sleep*, Sphere, 1982.

Murray, M. T., *Stress, Anxiety and Insomnia*, Prima, 1995. (Details of herb and food to aid sleep.)

O'Toole, Michael, *Living with Noises in your Head*, Souvenir Press, 1995.

Oswald, Professor Ian & Adam, Kirstine, PhD, *Get a Better Night's Sleep*, Optima, 1990.

Priest, R, *Anxiety and Depression: a Practical Guide to Recovery*, Macdonald Optima.

Robinson, Jane, *The Alternative & Complementary Health Compendium*, Millennium Profiles, 1996.

Sadler, Jan, *Natural Pain Relief – a Practical Handbook for Self-Help*, Element Books, 1997.

Shapiro, Colin, *Conquering Insomnia*, Empowering Press, 1994.

Tiserand, R., *Aromatherapy for Everyone*, Penguin Books, 1988.

Van Straten, Michael, *The Good Sleep Guide*, Kyle Cathie, 1990.

Weekes, Claire, *Self-Help for Your Nerves*, Angus & Robertson.

Useful Addresses

Please send large A4 sae if writing for information.

Association of Reflexologists,
27 Old Gloucester Street,
London WC1N 3XX

The British Association for
Counselling,
37a Sheep Street,
Rugby EV21 3BX

Sleep Assessment and Advisory
Service,
British Sleep Society, PO Box 21,
Enterprise Crescent, Lisburn,
N. Ireland

The British Snoring and Sleep
Apnoea Association,
The Steps, How Lane,
Chipstead,
Surrey CR5 3LT

CRUSE, Cruse House,
126 Sheen Road,
Richmond,
Surrey TW9 1UR
0181 940 4818 – (Counselling,
advice for bereaved people.)

Council for Involuntary
Tranquilliser Addiction (CITA),
Cavendish House,
Brighton Road, Waterloo,
Liverpool, L22 5NG
0151 949 0102

Marsona Europe,
PO Box 4027,
London SW6 2XW
0171 924 1955
Fax: 0171 924 6899 (Natural
Sound Machines to cover tinnitus)

Medical Advisory Service, Sleep
Matters,
PO Box 3087,
London W4 4ZP
Helpline: 0181 994 9874

MIND,
Granta House, 15/19 Broadway,
London E15
0181 519 2122
(Details of local tranquilliser with-
drawal support groups)
0235 660 163
(Information leaflets.)

Narcotics Anonymous,
PO Box 1980,
London N19 3LS
0171 498 9005 (helpline)
0171 272 9040 (general office)

National Institution of Medical
Herbalists,
Dept. H, 9 Palace Gate, Exeter,
EX1 1JA
0192 426 022

Relaxation for Living,
168-170 Oatlands Drive,
Weybridge, KT13 9ET
01932 858 355

RNID Tinnitus Helpline,
2 Pelham Court,
Pelham Road,
Nottingham, NG5 1AP
Tinnitus Helpline: 0345 090 201

Women's Nutritional Advisory
Service,
PO Box 268,
Lewes
BN7 2QN.
01273 487 366
(For a food and herbal approach)

Outside the UK

American Sleep Disorders
Association
Sleep Laboratory
St Boniface Research Centre
351 Tache Avenue
Winnipeg
Manitoba R2H 2A6
Tel: 001-204 237 2760

Australasian Sleep Association
Psychology Department
University of Melbourne
Parkville
Victoria 3052
Australia
Tel: 00 61 3 344 4000

European Sleep Research Society
IPM and Department for Stress
Research
Karolinska Institute
Box 60205
S-10401 Stockholm
Sweden
Tel: 00 46 8 7286400

The Peaceful Sleep Audiotape
by Jan Sadler

If you haven't already got it, here's your chance to order the outstanding audiotape which Jan Sadler recorded specially to accompany this book. Side One consists of various essential relaxing techniques which combine to form the Peaceful Sleep Bedtime Routine. On Side Two, Jan's soothing and relaxing voice leads you through the full Peaceful Sleep Bedtime Routine. This beautiful relaxation and visualisation allows you to drift gently and easily into a deep and peaceful sleep.

ORDER FORM

Name . . . .

Address. . . . .

. . . .

. . . .

. . . . .Post Code . . . .

Please send me . . . . copies of the Peaceful Sleep Audiotape at £7.95 per tape, including post and packing.

I enclose my cheque for £. . . . .

Please make cheques payable to **Gateway Books** and send your completed order form to:
The Hollies, Wellow, Bath, BA2 8QJ

For details of Jan Sadler's other tapes send a s.a.e. to her at:
1 Penoweth, Mylor Bridge, Falmouth, Cornwall TR11 5NQ.

Index